OUR SAVIOR'S LOVE

OUR
SAVIOR'S
Love

HOPE & HEALING IN CHRIST

ALONZO L. GASKILL
& STANLEY A. JOHNSON

EDITORS

RSC
BYU

DESERET
BOOK

Published by the Religious Studies Center, Brigham Young University, Provo, Utah, in cooperation with Deseret Book Company, Salt Lake City.
Visit us at rsc.byu.edu.

Printed in the United States of America by Sheridan Books, Inc.
22 21 20 19 18 17 16 15 14   1 2 3 4 5

Deseret Book is a registered trademark of Deseret Book Company.
Visit us at DeseretBook.com.

Frontispiece: Wilson J. Ong, *Resurrection*. Cover and interior design by Carmen Cole.

ISBN 978-0-8425-2883-2
US Retail: $17.99

Library of Congress Cataloging-in-Publication Data
BYU Easter Conference (2014 : Brigham Young University)
    Our Savior's love : hope & healing in Christ / Alonzo L. Gaskill
    and Stanley A. Johnson, editors.
        p.   cm.
    Includes bibliographical references and index.
    ISBN 978-0-8425-2883-2
    1. Jesus Christ--Mormon interpretations--Congresses. I. Gaskill,
Alonzo L., editor. II. Title.
BX8643.J4B97 2014
232.088'2893--dc23   2014037804

CONTENTS

INTRODUCTION

A t the core of the human experience is the ever-so-difficult task of seeing things "as they really are" (Jacob 4:13). And paramount in that process is discovering for oneself the reality of Christ's love and experiencing that love on a personal level. (Knowing the doctrine that he loves us is most certainly not the same as experiencing in one's own life the manifestation of that love.)

When the miracle happens—when we actually, really know, understand, and feel of *our Savior's love*—we are transformed; we are changed in our understanding of what that divine love is, but also changed in our nature and being because of what that love does to us. In so many ways, actually encountering our Savior's love

Left: Simon Vedder, Supper at Emmaus. *Courtesy of Church History Museum.*

chips away at that natural man which is an enemy of all righteousness (see Mosiah 3:19; Moroni 9:6). It is the encounter with God's love that causes us to desire—to desperately desire—to submit our wills and lives to God's will and way. And through that desire our lives can be filled with hope *in* him and healing *through* him who is mighty to save (see 2 Nephi 31:19; Alma 7:14). Elder Neal A. Maxwell explained, "Submissiveness involves an invitation to come to grips with reality—to come into harmony with 'things as they really are.' Only then, proceeding from where one now is, can genuine spiritual progress be made."[1] Indeed! And when we finally experience that sacred transition from an intellectual belief in God's love to an actual encounter with

When we finally experience that sacred transition from an intellectual belief in God's love to an actual encounter with our Savior's love, the natural result is a sacred concern for those whom God has placed in our midst.

our Savior's love, the natural result is a sacred concern for those whom God has placed in our midst. Elder Maxwell said, "When we see 'things as they really are,' we shall see others and ourselves as we really are."[2] And, like Enos of old, once we hear God's Spirit whisper, "Thy sins are forgiven thee" (Enos 1:5), our natural response is to "feel a desire for the welfare of" our brothers and sisters and to "pour out" our "whole soul unto God for them" (Enos 1:9). Our Savior's love enables us to see ourselves in proper perspective and thereby to see others as God sees them, and to love them as deeply as he loves them.

INTRODUCTION

In commemoration of God's ultimate act of adoration for his creations, we present to you these testaments of our Savior's love and their accompanying invitations to "come unto Christ, and be perfected in him . . . that by his grace ye may be perfect in Christ" (Moroni 10:32). May the perspectives and testimonies borne on the pages of this small book fill you with love—for God and for all of humanity. And may they inspire you to exercise hope in Christ that you might experience his healing influence in your life and convey that gift to all whom God places within your scope of influence.

Alonzo L. Gaskill and Stanley A. Johnson

NOTES

1. Neal A. Maxwell, *Even As I Am* (Salt Lake City: Deseret Book, 1982), 43.
2. Neal A. Maxwell, *All These Things Shall Give Thee Experience* (Salt Lake City: Deseret Book, 1980), 62.

ELDER SPENCER J. CONDIE

"HE LIVES TO BLESS ME WITH HIS LOVE"

There are dozens of inspiring sacred hymns which eloquently extol the divine attributes of the Son of God and testify of our Savior's love. One of these favorite hymns is Samuel Medley's "I Know That My Redeemer Lives,"[1] which enumerates many of the ways in which the Savior's love is manifest in each of our personal lives.

"HE LIVES TO BLESS ME WITH HIS LOVE"

In testimony meetings, faithful Saints often testify of occasions when they have strongly felt the Savior's love for them. "For God so loved the world, that he gave his only begotten Son, that whosoever believeth in him

ELDER SPENCER J. CONDIE is an emeritus member of the First Quorum of the Seventy.

should not perish, but have everlasting life. For God sent not his Son into the world to condemn the world; but that the world through him might be saved" (John 3:16–17).

It is true that the Savior of the world came to save us, *not* to condemn us. But saving us, sometimes from ourselves and our unwise actions, often requires chastening, as the Lord Himself explained: "Whom I love I also chasten that their sins may be forgiven, for with the chastisement I prepare a way for their deliverance in all things out of temptation, and I have loved you" (D&C 95:1).

Some Latter-day Saints do not fully understand the difference between condemnation and chastening, assuming the terms are equivalent. The adjective "chaste" is a synonym for "pure." Thus the verb "chasten" refers to the process of purification, *not* harsh criticism or condemnation. The late Elder Orson F. Whitney (1855–1931) captured this process well:

> Chasten my soul till I shall be
> In perfect harmony with thee.
> Make me more worthy of thy love,
> And fit me for the life above.[2]

The Savior's patient, persistent mentoring of the Apostle Peter exemplifies His love for Peter and is a metaphor for each of us. In preparing Peter eventually to lead the church after His Crucifixion, Resurrection, and Ascension into heaven, the Savior frequently chastened Peter as recorded throughout the four Gospels (see Matthew 14:31; 16:22; 26:34–41; Mark 14:37–38; Luke 22:31–32; John 13:4–9; 18:10; 21:15–22). In this last dispensation, the Lord chastened the Prophet Joseph Smith on various occasions, and Joseph humbly recorded these in the Doctrine and Covenants (see D&C 3:4–9; 5:21; 35:19; 93:47–49). Through the Lord's chastening, both Peter and Joseph did become more fit to lead the kingdom on earth. In both instances, a loving Savior showed forth greater love after the chastening (see Matthew 16:16–19; D&C 76:5; 110:5; 121:7).

The late Pierre Teilhard de Chardin asserted that "God must, in some way or other, make room for Himself, hollowing us out and emptying us."[3] A natural consequence of humbly accepting the Lord's chastening process is the acquisition of charity, which Mormon defines as "the pure love of Christ." Chastening provides the hollowing which precedes the hallowing described by Mormon as he explains how we can acquire charity in our lives. He admonishes us to "pray unto the Father with all the energy of heart, that [we] may be filled with this love, which he hath bestowed upon all who are true followers of his Son, Jesus Christ" (Moroni 7:48).

"I Feel My Savior's Love"[4] is a beautiful song and a source of inspiration reflecting how we can truly *feel* of that divine love. However, Mormon takes us one step further along the pathway to perfection. He admonishes us to "pray unto the Father with all the energy of heart, that [we] may be *filled* with this love" (emphasis added). There can be a great difference between *feeling* His love and being *filled* with His love. Those who have committed a grievous sin and confess it to their bishop, through the actions of their kindly priesthood leader, may *feel* of the Savior's love. But individuals who are *filled* with the Savior's love will not have committed the sin in the first place. When

3

one is filled with the pure love of Christ, there is no more room for anger, lust, hatred, discouragement, doubt or fear, pride, or envy because a heart full of love is *full*. We then become "settled" and "rooted and grounded in love" (Colossians 1:23; Ephesians 3:17).

In King Benjamin's benedictory sermon, he taught that "the natural man is an enemy to God" and that we can overcome the natural man by yielding "to the enticings of the Holy Spirit," becoming as a child, being "submissive, meek, humble, patient, *full of love*" (Mosiah 3:19; emphasis added).

> *When one is filled with the pure love of Christ, there is no more room for anger, lust, hatred, discouragement, doubt, or fear.*

Alma counseled his missionary son Shiblon, "Use boldness, but not overbearance; and also see that ye bridle all your passions, that ye may be *filled with love*" (Alma 38:12; emphasis added). When young missionaries' hearts are filled with love, distracting aspirations for leadership positions, intolerance of a companion's idiosyncrasies, and criticism of a new cultural environment evaporate as they focus all their efforts upon building the kingdom of God.

In Mormon's second epistle, he discusses the importance of baptism, the first fruits of repentance: "And the remission of sins bringeth meekness, and lowliness

---

of heart; and because of meekness and lowliness of heart cometh the visitation of the Holy Ghost, which Comforter *filleth with hope and perfect love*" (Moroni 8:26; emphasis added). Repentance is the hollowing process which precedes the hallowing of perfect love.

> *It was the Savior's perfect love for His Father, His perfect love for the plan of salvation, and His perfect love for all humankind which fortified Him for the terrible task ... of Gethsemane.*

It was the Savior's perfect love for His Father, His perfect love for the plan of salvation, and His perfect love for all humankind which fortified Him for the terrible task which lay before Him as He approached the Garden of Gethsemane. As He entered the garden, Mark records that He "began to be sore amazed, and to be very heavy [or in anguish]" (Mark 14:33). It was one thing to volunteer to fulfill the Father's plan as it was presented in the Council in Heaven, but now He had to face the painful reality that suffering for the sins of the world would cause even Him, the Son of God, "to tremble because of pain, and to bleed at every pore, and to suffer both body and spirit" (D&C 19:18).

President Gordon B. Hinckley declared, "There would be no Christmas if there had not been Easter. The babe Jesus of Bethlehem would be but another baby without the redeeming Christ of Gethsemane and Calvary, and the triumphant fact of the Resurrection."[5]

"He Lives to Bless Me with His Love"

"he lives to plead for me above"

As the Savior appeared in the Kirtland Temple the week after its dedication, He introduced Himself to Joseph and Oliver with this declaration: "I am the first and the last; I am he who liveth, I am he who was slain; *I am your advocate with the Father.*" Then, speaking as an advocate, He gave the Prophet and Oliver divine reassurance: "Behold, your sins are forgiven you; you are clean before me; therefore, lift up your heads and rejoice" (D&C 110:4–5; emphasis added; see also D&C 29:5).

An advocate is frequently seen as a lawyer who is retained to represent someone who has been injured by another person and seeks redress and compensation for his or her injuries. Advocates may also be hired to defend and plead the cause of someone guilty of wrongdoing or someone who, through no fault of their own, has fallen on hard times. For example, a married couple faced with unforeseen catastrophic medical expenses may have fallen in arrears in their mortgage payments, and the bank is preparing to take them to court prior to foreclosing their mortgage and evicting them from their home. A skillful advocate may be hired to convince the bank to allow the couple more time to arrange their financial affairs so as to honorably meet all their fiduciary obligations. But even if the bank does agree to delay the foreclosure and to lower the monthly payments, the couple will still receive a bill from their lawyer or advocate for services rendered.

The Savior's role as our Advocate with the Father follows a much different pattern. If the married couple facing a foreclosure of their house has honestly tried to live within their means, the Savior, as their Advocate, will not only forgo sending a bill for services, but He may actually pay the remaining debt they are unable to pay.

Father Lehi taught his son Jacob that Christ "shall make intercession for all the children of men; and they that believe in him shall be saved" (2 Nephi 2:9). Jacob later expanded upon his father's teaching as he declared, "The Lord and thy God pleadeth the cause of his people; behold, I have taken out of thine hand the cup of trembling, the dregs of the cup of my fury; thou shalt no more drink it again" (2 Nephi 8:22). We will never be able to repay Him for His atoning sacrifice as our Advocate with the Father, for "it is by grace that we are saved, after all we can do" (2 Nephi 25:23). "For he hath answered the ends of the law, and he claimeth all those who have faith in him; and they who have faith in him will cleave unto every good thing; wherefore he advocateth the cause of the children of men; and he dwelleth eternally in the heavens" (Moroni 7:28).

"HE LIVES MY HUNGRY SOUL TO FEED"

There are many different objects of hunger in addition to food. Parents of missionaries may hunger for an e-mail assuring them their favorite missionary is doing well. Lonely widows hunger for an occasional visit from their children and grandchildren. Then there is the hunger for the word of God. In the sermon at the temple given to the Nephites, the Savior said, "And blessed are all they who do hunger and thirst after righteousness, for they shall be filled with the Holy Ghost" (3 Nephi 12:6).

I was impressed by the Czechoslovakian Saints and their hunger and thirsting for the things of righteousness. Five years before the demise of communism, the Czechoslovakian Soviet Socialist Republic exercised tight restrictions on religious materials. The Czech Book of Mormon was printed the size of a pocket hymnbook so men could carry it unobtrusively in a suit pocket and women could fit their book into a small purse.

When we would go to Czechoslovakia to meet with the Saints, I would evenly distribute half a dozen copies of the Book of Mormon under my shirt and then button up my vest and suit coat. Dorothea would put some books in the bottom of her knitting bag and then cover them with a partially knit sweater with the sharp ends of the needles pointed upward.

Upon arrival at the district president's home, we were greeted with the anxious question "What were you able to bring?" These Saints truly hungered and thirsted after the things of righteousness, and each printed page of scripture or the words of the living prophets were pure gold to them.

The Book of Mormon: Another Testament of Jesus Christ in Czech. © by Intellectual Reserve, Inc.

In the very first chapter of the Book of Mormon, Nephi recounts a vision Father Lehi had as he beheld "One descending out of the midst of heaven" with "twelve others following."

"And they came down and went forth upon the face of the earth; and the first came and stood before my father, and gave unto him a book, and bade him that he should read. And it came to pass that *as he read, he was filled with the Spirit of the Lord*" (1 Nephi 1:9–12; emphasis added). Lehi did not just *feel* the Spirit as he read; rather, he was *filled* with the Spirit of the Lord.

In addition to searching the scriptures, another means of filling our spiritual hunger is through making covenants and participating in the ordinances of the priesthood, for the Lord revealed that it is through the ordinances of the priesthood that the power of godliness is manifest to men in the flesh (see D&C 84:19–21). Elder Melvin J. Ballard (1873–1939) posed the introspective question "How can we have *spiritual* hunger? Who is there among us that does not wound his spirit by word, thought, or deed, from Sabbath to Sabbath?" He continues: "I am a witness that there is a spirit attending the administration of the sacrament that warms the soul from head to foot; you feel the wounds of the spirit being healed, and the load being lifted. Comfort and happiness come to the soul that is worthy and truly desirous of partaking of this spiritual food."[6]

"HE LIVES TO BLESS IN TIME OF NEED"

Elder David A. Bednar's parable of the pickup truck, told in the April 2014 general conference, is a classic example of receiving a blessing in time of need. You recall that Elder Bednar's friend "decided he would cut and haul a supply of firewood for their home. It was in the autumn of the year, and snow already had fallen in the mountains where he intended to find wood. As he drove up the mountainside, the snow gradually became deeper and deeper," and he eventually became hopelessly stuck in the deep snow.

Rather than just sitting and waiting for help to come, he started cutting wood and loading it into the truck until "he completely filled the back of the truck with the heavy load." He then decided to try driving through the deep snow one more time. He was surprised to discover that as he started his truck and gave it some gas, it gradually began moving through the deep snow back onto the road, homeward bound.

Likening this experience to the circumstances in our life, Elder Bednar suggested that each of us ask the introspective question "Is the load I am carrying producing the spiritual traction that will enable me to press forward with faith in Christ on the strait and narrow path and avoid getting stuck?"[7]

We often pray with an expectation that our supplication will be answered in a certain preconceived manner, but in many instances the Lord's tender mercies are granted not in terms of what we want, but rather in terms of what we need at a given time. It is always important to ensure that our heavy loads provide us with increasing spiritual traction.

"HE LIVES TO SILENCE ALL MY FEARS . . .
[AND] WIPE AWAY MY TEARS"

The greatest fear I have ever seen, greater than a long list of phobias I have observed in various people, is the fear that one's eternal exaltation has been everlastingly lost. Several years ago I received the assignment to interview an elderly sister while visiting a stake conference in northern Europe. She had been excommunicated more than twenty years previously, and during the past year she had been re-baptized. She had now been recommended by her bishop and her stake president as one worthy to receive the restoration of her temple blessings pending a satisfactory interview with a General Authority.

I called to make an appointment to visit with her before or after the various stake conference meetings, which would be held in a couple of months. I was surprised at her response. She asked, "Do you realize that I am eighty-three years of age and I may not be here in several weeks? Are you going to be in your office in Frankfurt tomorrow?" I replied in the affirmative, and she responded, "I will take the morning train and be in Frankfurt tomorrow afternoon, and I will come directly to your office."

True to her word, at 4:00 p.m. this frail little lady with flushed cheeks and her hair in a bun entered my office huffing and puffing. After catching her breath and regaining her composure, we began to discuss her past life and the circumstances leading to our interview together. Twenty-five years previously, her husband, who was a rather large man, became seriously ill and needed a great deal of care over a considerable length of time. She had a good neighbor about her age who generously offered to help her care for her husband, especially when he needed to be bathed or she needed to change the bedsheets.

This kind neighbor was the epitome of a good Samaritan. But one day, in an unguarded moment, as the woman began to express her heartfelt gratitude for his countless acts of kindness, the two of them let down their guard and expressed their mutual affection far beyond the bounds of propriety. Shortly thereafter she met with her bishop to confess her transgression, and a disciplinary council was held with a decision of excommunication.

Her understanding of excommunication was that once she had lost her membership in the Church she would be completely ostracized for the rest of her life. Her hope of exaltation in the celestial kingdom seemed to be no longer possible. For the next twenty-three years, she languished in loneliness with an unrelenting fear of dying unfit for the celestial kingdom.

She never visited a church meeting, and not once did she receive visits from visiting teachers, home teachers, or the bishopric. "Then," she said, "two years ago two young men came to visit me and explained they were my home teachers and had been assigned to bring me back into the fold." She became teary-eyed as she said, "I was so glad to see them I nearly fell upon their necks and kissed both of them." Since that first visit she had regularly attended all of her meetings and had meticulously kept all the commandments.

After our interview, the Spirit confirmed that she should, indeed, receive a restoration of her long-awaited temple blessings. When I removed my hands from her head, I said, "Now the next time your stake has a temple trip to Frankfurt, you'll want to be certain to participate with them." She responded: "You seem to forget how old

I am. I may not be here for the next temple trip. I antici-
pated going to the temple tomorrow." I called the temple
president and arranged for her to participate in several ordinances in the Frankfurt temple before returning home.
The Savior's redeeming love had, indeed, silenced all her
fears and wiped away her tears.

"HE LIVES TO CALM MY TROUBLED HEART"

Several years ago my home teaching companion and
I were in the middle of a visit to one of our ward families
during the Christmas season. Suddenly we were startled to
see one of their teenage sons burst through the door with
his lower arm bound with a cloth to staunch the bleeding
from a large cut on his wrist. This was their problem child
who had become addicted to drugs. He was obviously high
on drugs as he proceeded to knock over the decorated
Christmas tree and began stomping on all the ornaments
while profaning in the most blasphemous terms the name
of Deity. He then castigated his father in vile language
and then called his mother the most disparaging names
imaginable.

We felt prompted to invoke the power of the priesthood to command Satan to depart from that home, and
the young man suddenly left. The parents were devastated,
embarrassed, and humiliated at their son's actions, especially in the presence of home teachers. They contritely
confessed their failure as parents and hoped the Lord
would forgive them for their inadequacies.

We asked them, "When was the last time you attended the temple?' They responded, "How can we go to the temple when we have this kind of a spirit in our home?" We ascertained that they both held current recommends and then, once again, urged them to go to the temple.

The next week we dropped by to see how things were going in their home. Their son had been arrested and was consigned to a strict rehabilitation program, and there was a ray of hope in their lives.

They then described the sweet, calming spirit they felt during their recent visit to the temple. The mother said, "They even invited us to be the witness couple." Then, with tears coursing down her cheeks, she said, "Maybe that's a sign that Heavenly Father hasn't given up on us after all." Being filled with the Spirit in the temple, feelings of self-doubt and shame were replaced by a love of their son as seen through the eyes of a Savior who loved him enough to die for him. They had learned that the holy temple is not just a place of sealing but also a place of healing.

They had learned that the holy temple is not just a place of sealing but also a place of healing.

The hollowing of our lives prepares us for the hallowing that comes from our Savior's love as we begin to emulate Him. The empty tomb that first Easter morning is a poignant metaphor of the hollowing which precedes the hallowing: "the will of the Son being swallowed up in the will of the Father" (Mosiah 15:7).

The Savior testified, "I am come that they might have life, and that they might have it more abundantly" (John 10:10). His entire gospel radiates abundance rather than scarcity, inclusion rather than exclusion. We truly live in the dispensation of the *fulness* of times.

In the inspiring discourse on faith, the author of Hebrews refers to the great faith of Abel, Enoch, Noah, Abraham, and Sarah and concludes, "These all died in faith, not having received the promises, but having seen them afar off, and were persuaded of them, and embraced them" (Hebrews 11:13).

The Savior reminded those who had observed His many miracles and had heard His inspiring sermons that "many prophets and righteous men have desired to see those things which ye see, and have not seen them; and to hear those things which ye hear, and have not heard them" (Matthew 13:17). We have lived to see the unfolding of this promise.

As the Savior prepared His disciples for His impending departure, He promised them that "He that believeth on me, the works that I do shall he do also; and *greater works than these shall he do*; because I go unto my Father" (John 14:12; emphasis added). When the Savior prophesied that His disciples would do even greater works than He, this may have been true in terms of numbers of convert baptisms and the number of temple ordinances performed,

---

but let us never forget that He created the earth under the direction of the Father and that He holds the keys of the Resurrection.

The infinite love and trust of the Father and the Son is manifest by sharing their priesthood power and authority of "the Holy Priesthood, after the Order of the Son of God" with imperfect men on earth (D&C 107:3). Worthy men have been authorized to perform sacred ordinances with the promise to all who become pure and remain faithful that "*all that my Father hath shall be given unto [them]*" (D&C 84:38; emphasis added). It is through the ordinances of the holy priesthood that "the power of godliness is manifest . . . unto men in the flesh" (D&C 84:19–21). Through the performing and receiving of holy ordinances heaven draws nearer to earth, if you will, and by keeping the covenants inherent in these ordinances, we are edified and purified.

Many of these sacred ordinances are performed only in the house of the Lord, and His invitation is extended to all to repent and to become worthy to enter His holy house to receive life-saving ordinances for themselves and to perform these ordinances vicariously for those who have passed beyond. The author of Hebrews wrote that Christ "obtained a more excellent ministry, by how much also he is the mediator of a *better covenant,* which was *established upon better promises*" (Hebrews 8:6; emphasis added).

Left: The Frankfurt Germany Temple. © by Intellectual Reserve, Inc.

Those better covenants and better promises are made in a holy temple, a place of sealing and a place of healing.

The ordinances of the restored gospel, including the new and everlasting covenant, not only bind us together as families for eternity, but they also help to purify us as we renew our covenants in sacred precincts. Thus, when promises and covenants are kept, the ordinances of the gospel perform a kind of divine dialysis, removing the taint of worldliness from our lives by providing celestial cleansing and spiritual renewal.

Moroni concludes the record of his father, Mormon, with the promise that "whoso receiveth this record, and shall not condemn it because of the imperfections which are in it, *the same shall know of greater things than these*" (Mormon 8:12; emphasis added). Notwithstanding the fulness contained in the Book of Mormon, a loving Savior revealed to the Prophet Joseph additional inspiring revelations contained in the Doctrine and Covenants and the Pearl of Great Price, ever expanding our knowledge of the gospel and the plan of salvation.

The Lord's blessing for paying our tithing is but another example of the abundant life in which He promised to open "the windows of heaven, and pour you out a blessing, that there shall not be room enough to receive it" (Malachi 3:10). And to those who keep their temple covenants faithfully, the promise is given that the glory they receive "shall be a fulness and a continuation of the seeds forever and ever" (D&C 132:19).

"He Lives to Bless Me with His Love"

"He Lives and Grants Me Daily Breath"

During an earlier reading of the Book of Mormon, I confess that I was slightly doubtful of King Benjamin's promise that if we are obedient to all the Lord's commandments, "he doth immediately bless you," "preserving you from day to day, by lending you breath" (Mosiah 2:24, 21).

I was a healthy young lad when I first read that passage, and my eyes and my mind focused upon the phrase "he doth immediately bless you." At the time I considered that promise to be a bit extravagant; however, over the years I have become acquainted with many faithful Saints who suffer severe respiratory problems or congestive heart failure that requires them to have the continuous support of an oxygen tank. With overwhelming gratitude, these faithful folks understand the promise that the Lord immediately blesses the righteous by "preserving [them] from day to day, by lending [them] breath" (Mosiah 2:21).

Those who daily suffer from various infirmities may take great comfort from Alma's prophecy regarding the Savior's infinite Atonement: "And he will take upon him death, that he may loose the bands of death which bind his people; and he will *take upon him their infirmities*" (Alma 7:12; emphasis added). Elder Bruce C. Hafen reminds us that "the Atonement is not just for sinners."[8]

"He Lives, and I Shall Conquer Death"

Karen is one of our good neighbors, and she is in her late seventies. Her first husband passed away about a dozen years ago after having served faithfully as a bishop. A couple of years later she married another neighbor,

Gary, who had lost his wife, and these two newlyweds accepted a mission call to serve throughout the South Pacific as family history missionaries. Their positive impact will be felt throughout the eternities.

While on their mission, Karen experienced some disconcerting medical symptoms, and after they returned home she was diagnosed with a serious liver ailment. Last August her physician told her, "Karen, your liver is shrinking to the size of a baseball, and your blood tests indicate some serious problems." His countenance then became very solemn as he continued, "I think you'll be fortunate if you are still around by year's end."

Given this prognosis, the doctor was astounded when Karen reacted with cheerful enthusiasm: "That's okay. I've paid for the burial plot, I've paid for the casket, and I've planned my funeral!" Her physician exclaimed, "Karen, did you hear what I said? You are probably going to pass away during the next four months!" "I'm at peace," she quietly replied.

A few weeks after her doctor's appointment, she related this conversation to us and testified that her unshakable testimony of the Resurrection and her undeniable witness of the temple sealing to her first husband had fully insulated her from all feelings of anxiety and fear. With peace that "passeth human understanding" she could proclaim with certitude: "O death, where is thy sting? O grave, where is thy victory?" (1 Corinthians 15:55–56).

"He Lives to Bless Me with His Love"

"he lives my mansion to prepare . . . [and] to bring me safely there"

In 1984 the Austria Vienna Mission included the countries of Greece, Czechoslovakia, Poland, Hungary, and Yugoslavia, where the district president was the Yugoslavian national basketball hero Kresimir Cosic. As a young man at six feet eleven inches tall, Kreso had bedaz-zled fans throughout Europe with his extraordinary basketball skills. Then in 1970, through a series of modern miracles, this twenty-two-year-old atheist arrived in Provo, Utah, to play basketball for the Brigham Young University Cougars.

Hugh Nibley and Kresimir Cosic. Screenshot courtesy of Deseret News.

A fellow Yugoslavian had come to BYU to play tennis and had befriended Christina Nibley. She, in turn, became acquainted with Kreso, and before long she had invited him to meet her famous father, Hugh. Though Kreso was still struggling with English, Hugh Nibley patiently began teaching him the gospel, and it became readily apparent that Kreso was no ordinary athlete. His perceptive questions reflected a sincere and unquenchable quest for gospel knowledge. In due time he was baptized by Hugh Nibley, and shortly thereafter Truman and Ann Madsen began to fellowship him and strengthen his testimony.

Sometime after Kreso's baptism, Hugh Nibley did something he had never done before. Instead of meeting in the Nibley home or in Brother Nibley's office, Brother Hugh knocked on the door of Kreso's apartment. Brother

Nibley's countenance was solemn as he began to explain that, as a young missionary in Germany in 1930 while waiting on a train platform, he gained a glimpse of the premortal existence. In that vision he participated in a council meeting in a large room in which the participants surrounded a large table. At the end of the table was a certain individual, and Hugh was given to understand that he would have the responsibility of assuring that that particular person had an opportunity to hear the gospel on earth.

With some emotion, Hugh Nibley disclosed that Kresimir Cosic was that man for whom he was given responsibility. He conceded that he had not recognized him at first, but after they became well acquainted, Kreso said, "He told me it was no coincidence that we knew one another."[9]

The baptism of Kresimir Cosic was not just the baptism of one individual, but what President Monson called the key to opening the country of Yugoslavia to the preaching of the gospel. After an extraordinary college career at BYU, Kreso was given lucrative offers to play in the NBA, but he declined these offers outright because he felt a compelling need to return to his homeland and to use his basketball stardom as a means of introducing the gospel to his native countrymen.

We often sing these familiar phrases and apply them only to *our* personal lives: "He lives *my* mansion to prepare. He lives to bring *me* safely there." In our Father's

---

Right: Yugoslavian national basketball hero Kresimir Cosic played for Brigham Young University. Courtesy of BYU Archives.

house are many mansions, and He has provided sacred ordinances to help order our lives and prepare us to follow the pathway to perfection back into His presence. But each of us has an obligation to assure that those around us also receive the same opportunity we have received, and we are obligated to help prepare others and "bring *them* safely there." Kreso understood this as he returned home.

In 2 Nephi the Lord declares two times: "I am able to do mine own work" (2 Nephi 27:20–21). He is, indeed, able to do His work without any help from us, but because He and His Father desire to have us grow and develop and become like Them, each of us is invited to assist Them in bringing to pass the immortality and eternal life of all of our Heavenly Father's children. "God so loved the world, that he gave his only begotten Son, that whosoever believeth in him should not perish, but have everlasting life" (John 3:16). "Greater love hath no man than this, that a man lay down his life for his friends" (John 15:13).

I know that my Redeemer lives and loves each of us.

NOTES

1. Samuel Medley, "I Know That My Redeemer Lives," *Hymns* (Salt Lake City: The Church of Jesus Christ of Latter-day Saints, 1985), no. 136.

2. Orson F. Whitney, "Savior, Redeemer of My Soul," *Hymns*, no. 112.

3. Pierre Teilhard de Chardin, *The Divine Milieu: An Essay on the Interior Life* (New York: Harper and Bros., 1960), 35.

4. Ralph Rodgers Jr., K. Newell Dayley, and Laurie Huffman, "I Feel My Savior's Love," *Children's Songbook* (Salt Lake City: The Church of Jesus Christ of Latter-day Saints), 74–75.

5. Gordon B. Hinckley, "The Wondrous and True Story of Christmas," *Ensign*, December 2000, 5.

6. Melvin Joseph Ballard, *Melvin J. Ballard: Crusader for Righteousness* (Salt Lake City: Bookcraft, 1966), 132–33.

7. David A. Bednar, "'Bear Up Their Burdens with Ease,'" *Ensign*, May 2014, 88.

8. Bruce C. Hafen, "Beauty for Ashes: The Atonement of Jesus Christ," *Ensign*, April 1990, 10.

9. Beverly B. Campbell, *Kresimir Cosic: One Man's Spiritual Journey* (Provo, UT: Y Mountain Press, 2014), 32–33.

"I Stand All Amazed"

In one of my favorite hymns about the Savior, the first line says, "I stand all amazed at the *love* Jesus offers me."[1] As I contemplate the Savior's matchless life, His mission, and His ministry, truly I do stand all amazed at His love, His life, and His infinite Atonement for you and for me. I stand all amazed at His ability to come to earth and show us what to do, to mark the path and show the way to become like Him, and to enable us to return back into our Heavenly Father's presence proven, pure, and sealed in holy temples as eternal families.

If I could add verses to this hymn, I would also say, I stand all amazed not only at His love but at His condescension, His patience, His humility, His self-control,

---

SISTER ELAINE S. DALTON is the former Young Women general president.

His focus, His desire to serve, His ability to teach and reach the one, His miracles, and His ability to bear our sins, sorrows, suffering, and imperfections. I stand all amazed at His matchless devotion and love for His Father, His virtue and purity, and the virtue of His infinite Atonement. And yes, I am "confused at the grace that so fully he proffers me,"[2] which is an enabling power that makes it possible to have strength, abilities, and power beyond my own.

Yes, I truly do stand all amazed!

LOVE

Frequently I ponder the same question that has been asked by others,[3] which is not *how* did he do it, but *why* did he do it? In the Grand Councils of Heaven, as the Firstborn of the Father, He volunteered, saying simply, "Here am I; send me."[4] Why? What prompted Him to volunteer? What desire, relationship, or gain?

> *The Firstborn of the Father, He volunteered, saying simply, "Here am I; send me." Why? What prompted Him to volunteer?*

As I have pondered His life, His ministry, and His mission, the *why* becomes clear. Everything He did was motivated by one thing—and one thing only. It was and is *love.* He was not motivated by power, position, or possessions. His motive was not political, and it was not to seek popularity. His motive was pure. He was motivated by *pure love.* He never betrayed His Father or our faith in Him, although he was betrayed because of His love for Heavenly

30

Father and us. He gave us reason to hope. He taught us through His actions about a different kind of love—charity, the pure love of Christ.[5] He could offer that kind of love only because He was pure in His motives, in His actions, and in His love. And though He was despised for it, He went about doing good because He was good.[6] He used His priesthood power to heal the sick and cause the lame to walk,[7] to discern, to bless, to teach, and to draw us close to Him. Through this power, He performed miracles. He raised the dead. He changed water to wine. He fed five thousand with five loaves and two fishes. His love for the Father and for us was pure—no motives, no agendas. He simply declared, "I and my Father are one."[8] "And He that sent me is with me: the Father hath not left me alone; for I do always those things that please him."[9] He loved us as His Father loved us: "For God so loved the world, that he gave his only begotten Son, that whosoever believeth in him should . . . have everlasting life."[10] In the world in which we live, with the motives and forces that work in the world, this truly unique attitude and approach is cause for each of us, even *all*, to stand all amazed. Do we always do those things that please the Father? How can we too become one with the Savior and the Father?

ATONEMENT

On a crisp fall morning, the day before Thanksgiving several years ago, I came to more deeply understand the Savior's love and the individual nature of His infinite Atonement. Early that morning, I went on a run with several friends. We called it our "thankful run." As we ran that morning, we called out randomly the things for which we were thankful. The air was crisp. It had snowed lightly and the world was spectacular; it was an ideal morning to run, and feelings of gratitude rushed over me as I did so. I had just finished calling out that I was thankful for a strong, healthy body when I stepped on a patch of black ice, hidden by the skiff of snow. I slipped, and before I knew it, I found myself lying on the road. As I tried to stand up, I realized that I had broken my leg just above the ankle. I won't attempt to describe to you how I knew. But later my husband said that if I had been a football player, I would have made the NFL highlight films that evening on television.

As I lay on the road, holding my leg so it wouldn't move, the pain was unbearable, and I was afraid I was going to faint. My friends ran to the nearest house with a light on and called my husband, who came immediately in the car. When I was loaded into my husband's car to be driven to the emergency room, one of my friends asked me what she could do to ease the pain. I asked her to sing to me. She began to sing, "I know that my Redeemer lives. What comfort this sweet sentence gives! . . . He lives to comfort me when faint. He lives to hear my soul's complaint. He lives to silence all my fears. He lives to wipe away my tears. He lives to calm my troubled heart. He lives all blessings to impart."[11]

When I heard those words, everything changed. He was right there with me and He bore my pain. At that moment, I knew—I knew I was not alone. I knew *He* knew. And I knew that through priesthood power and blessings and through His infinite Atonement, I would be all right.

After I arrived at the emergency room at the hospital, I received a priesthood blessing from my husband and our five sons and was taken into surgery. When I was sent home, I was given numerous medications for pain. But I never felt any pain. I spent weeks in bed healing, and that could have posed a trial to one who is so used to being active. But I have to tell you that I would not trade that experience or those weeks when I was "broken" and "still" for anything because of the sweet spiritual experiences I had and the sure knowledge I gained of our Savior, of His love, and of the healing and enabling power of His Atonement.

I testify that through His infinite Atonement, broken things can mend— broken hearts, broken lives, broken bodies, and broken dreams.

That day several years ago, while lying in the road in pain, I felt broken. Have any of you ever felt broken, perhaps with a broken heart after having broken commandments? Have any of you experienced broken dreams, broken relationships, a broken spirit? I testify, He is there to heal us, to bear our pain, and to enable us to bear all things. I testify that through His infinite Atonement, broken things can mend—broken hearts, broken lives, broken bodies, and broken dreams.

Through this experience, I realized that this is why He invites us to take His yoke upon us. He invites and reminds us, saying, "Come unto me, all ye that labour and are heavy laden, and I will give you rest. Take my yoke upon you. . . .

For my yoke is easy, and my burden is light."[12] And that day and since, I learned that His words are true because it is He that is on the other side of that yoke. And because He bore all things, He enables us to do the same. He strengthens us. He strengthened me. This is the enabling power of His Atonement. And I testify it is real. Yes, I stand all amazed at the grace that so fully He proffers me.

My desire from that time forth has been singular—to show my love to Him in all I do—to serve Him; to become like Him; to be His hands, His smile, His disciple. My desire is to help those who feel "broken" know that we do not ever walk alone—that the Savior is right there beside us. My desire is to help others know that even when we *feel* alone, He is *always* there. That is my *sure* knowledge. And yes, "I stand all amazed."[13]

Recently I visited Liberty Jail. There in that temple jail I once again stood all amazed as I recalled the feelings of Joseph Smith, whose intimate association with the Savior did not spare him suffering or injustice. Even with that kind of experience, knowledge, and commitment in his heart, Joseph cried to the Lord from the darkness and uncertainty of Liberty Jail, "O God, where art thou? And where is the pavilion that covereth thy hiding place? How long shall thy hand be stayed, and thine eye, yea thy pure eye, behold from the eternal heavens the wrongs of thy people and of thy servants, and thine ear be penetrated with their cries?"[14]

Right: Liz Lemon Swindle, Of One Heart, Joseph in Liberty Jail.
Courtesy of Foundation Arts.

have to be here, nor did he need to take his place on the stand. The entire congregation seemed to be in awe of his effort to perform his duty of being where he was supposed to be. Tears flowed freely as I watched him and the Spirit whispered, *Here is an example of humility*. This was one of those precious, parabolic moments, filled with customized tutoring in response to heartfelt need.

In that moment, I had a clear view of myself in the true light of the Son. I could see more of my potential to be a dutiful disciple. The Spirit testified a simple truth to me: perform your duty in humility. Here was an example of an offering of a broken heart and contrite spirit. I was changed by the example of another.

My friend died a few weeks later. At the viewing prior to the funeral service, his wife told me that he had awoken that morning with a desire to bear his testimony. While the opportunity to stand and testify with words was not granted, he testified to all of us that day in his deeds.

This man exemplified his love for the Lord through his actions, reminding us that the Savior wants us to know him. Christ invites us to come quickly unto him. His love casts darkness away. We are protected from deception when we choose to walk in his light as we see ourselves as we really are and as we really can be. This true, honest, penetrating light shows us the truth of all things. Indeed, "our Savior's love shines like the sun with perfect light." He lights our way, leading us back into his sight, to share eternal life.[44]

Left: Robert Barrett, Christ Healing the Man with the Withered Hand.
© *by Intellectual Reserve, Inc.*

NOTES

1. See, for instance, the chief priests and elders questioning the Lord's authority in Matthew 21:23, followed by three parables in response. Then Jesus denounces hypocrisy in Matthew 23.

2. Matthew chapter 24 and Joseph Smith—Matthew expound upon the signs given by the Savior in response to his disciple's inquiry as to what the signs of our Lord's coming will be.

3. Joseph Smith—Matthew 1:22.

4. Matthew 22:42.

5. D&C 52:14.

6. D&C 52:15–17.

7. Edward L. Hart and Crawford Gates, interview on the Mormon Channel, "Our Savior's Love," http://www .mormonchannel.org/history-of-hymns/20.

8. M. Russell Ballard, "Following Up," *Ensign*, April 2014, 79.

9. *Preach My Gospel: A Guide to Missionary Service* (Salt Lake City: The Church of Jesus Christ of Latter-day Saints, 2004), 115–26.

10. A careful study of the teaching resource *Teaching, No Greater Call* provides greater insight into teaching methods of the Lord. Additionally, Robert J. Matthews has a thorough treatment of many of the Savior's teaching methods in his book *A Bible! A Bible!* (Salt Lake City: Bookcraft, 1990).

11. Christ came into the world not only to atone for the sins of mankind but also to set an example before the world of the standard of perfection of God's law and of obedience to the Father. In his Sermon on the Mount, the Master has given us somewhat of a revelation of his own character, which was perfect, or what might be said to be "an autobiography, every syllable of which he had written down in deeds," and in so doing has given

us a blueprint for our own lives. Harold B. Lee, *Decisions for Successful Living* (Salt Lake City: Deseret Book, 1974), 55–56.

12. D. Kelly Ogden and Andrew C. Skinner, *Verse by Verse, The Four Gospels* (Salt Lake City: Deseret Book, 2006), 766; see also LDS Bible Dictionary, "Feasts," 673.

13. John 8:12.

14. Matthew 5:14–16.

15. See LDS Bible Dictionary, "Parables," 740–41.

16. See 3 Nephi 27:14–15.

17. Alonzo L. Gaskill, *Sacred Symbols: Finding Meaning in Rites, Ritual, and Ordinances* (Springville, UT: Cedar Fort, 2011), 2.

18. Dr. Fiese is a professor of human development and family studies. She focuses on the role of routine and ritual in family life, particularly the family mealtime. See Barbara H. Fiese, *Family Routines and Rituals* (New Haven, CT: Yale University Press, 2006).

19. For further discussion on the application and implication of ritual, see Jennifer A. Brinkerhoff, "Being a Good Ethiopian Woman: Participation in the 'Buna' (Coffee) Ceremony and Identity" (PhD diss., Arizona State University, 2011), and Jennifer Brinkerhoff Platt, *Living Your Covenants Every Day* (Salt Lake City: Deseret Book, 2013).

20. See Mark 14:15 and Luke 17:8.

21. Psalm 81:8–13.

22. Psalm 118:25–26.

23. Bruce R. McConkie, *The Mortal Messiah: From Bethlehem to Calvary*, 4 vols. (Salt Lake City: Deseret Book, 1981), 4:29.

24. Amulek teaches the apostate Zoramites of the need for an atonement in Alma chapter 34. The passage quoted here is found in verse 15.

25. Discipleship is evidenced by the way we love one another: "A new commandment I give unto you, That ye love one another; as I have loved you, that ye also love one another. By this shall all men know that ye are my disciples, if ye have love one to another" (John 13:34–35).

26. The disciples had associated with the Lord for three years. And for reasons we do not know, "the Holy Ghost did not operate in the fullness among the Jews during the years of Jesus' mortal sojourn." LDS Bible Dictionary, "Holy Ghost," 704. This promise of continual companionship allowed the disciples to walk by faith, with an unseen member of the Godhead at their side. It is as if the Lord is saying that they are not intended to be comfortable but that they will be comforted with the assistance of the Comforter. "But the Comforter, which is the Holy Ghost, whom the Father will send in my name, he shall teach you all things, and bring all things to your remembrance, whatsoever I have said unto you" (John 14:26).

27. The Lord assures them, "Abide in me, and I in you. As the branch cannot bear fruit of itself, except it abide in the vine; no more can ye, except ye abide in me. I am the vine, ye are the branches: He that abideth in me, and I in him, the same bringeth forth much fruit: for without me ye can do nothing" (John 15:4–5).

28. As a symbol of the fruitlessness of Israel, the Lord curses a fig tree to demonstrate his power while teaching the necessity of doing more than appearing to be committed but rather doing good works. See Matthew 21:17–21.

29. See John 17.

30. Elder Neal A. Maxwell said: "Later, in Gethsemane, the suffering Jesus began to be 'sore amazed' (Mark 14:33), or, in the Greek, 'awestruck' and 'astonished.' Imagine, Jehovah, the Creator of this and other worlds, 'astonished'! Jesus knew

cognitively what He must do, but not experientially. He had never personally known the exquisite and exacting process of an atonement before. Thus, when the agony came in its fulness, it was so much, much worse than even He with his unique intellect had ever imagined! No wonder an angel appeared to strengthen him! (See Luke 22:43.) The cumulative weight of all mortal sins—past, present, and future—pressed upon that perfect, sinless, and sensitive Soul! All our infirmities and sicknesses were somehow, too, a part of the awful arithmetic of the Atonement. (See Alma 7:11–12; Isaiah 53:3–5; Matthew 8:17.) The anguished Jesus not only pled with the Father that the hour and cup might pass from Him, but with this relevant citation. 'And he said, Abba, Father, all things are possible unto thee; take away this cup from me.' (Mark 14:35–36.)" Neal A. Maxwell, "Willing to Submit," *Ensign*, May 1985, 72–73.

31. See Alma 7:12.

32. James E. Talmage explains, "It seems, that in addition to the fearful suffering incident to crucifixion, the agony of Gethsemane had recurred, intensified beyond human power to endure." James E. Talmage, *Jesus the Christ*, 3rd ed. (Salt Lake City: The Church of Jesus Christ of Latter-day Saints, 1916), 661. Additionally, Elder Bruce R. McConkie said, "All of the anguish, all of the sorrow, and all of the suffering of Gethsemane recurred during the final three hours on the cross." McConkie, *Mortal Messiah*, 4:232.

33. Talmage, *Jesus the Christ*, 661.

34. Isaiah 63:3.

35. Jeffrey R. Holland, "'This Do in Remembrance of Me,'" *Ensign*, November 1995, 68.

36. President Smith reminds us that "our faith is always measured by our works. If we fully appreciated the many

blessings which are ours through the redemption made for us, there is nothing that the Lord could ask of us that we would not anxiously and willingly do." Joseph Fielding Smith, *Doctrines of Salvation*, comp. Bruce R. McConkie (Salt Lake City: Bookcraft, 1955), 346.

37. Smith, *Doctrines of Salvation*, 346.

38. Russell M. Nelson, "Worshiping at Sacrament Meeting," *Ensign*, August 2004, 26–27.

39. David A. Bednar, "Quick to Observe," *Brigham Young University Speeches, 2005–2006* (Provo, UT: Intellectual Reserve, Inc., 2006).

40. See Joachim Neander, "Praise to the Lord, the Almighty," *Hymns* (Salt Lake City: The Church of Jesus Christ of Latter-day Saints, 1985), no. 72.

41. See Moroni 4 and 5; D&C 20:77, 79.

42. John 14:26–27.

43. Mabel Jones Gabbott, "In Humility, Our Savior," *Hymns*, no. 172.

44. See Edward L. Hart, "Our Savior's Love," *Hymns*, no. 113.

INDEX

I suppose there has been or will be times in our lives when we too will cry out in prayer, perhaps asking some of the same questions. There will be times when we too feel abandoned, isolated, helpless, hopeless, or alone. At these times, the very fact that the Lord responded is a testament to me that we really are never alone. The Lord knows us. He is there. His response to Joseph tutors each of us: "My son, peace be unto thy soul; thine adversity and thine afflictions shall be but a small moment; and then, if thou endure it well, God shall exalt thee on high; thou shalt triumph over all thy foes."[15] If thou endure it well!

As the Savior taught us by His example, the most important thing we can do when unexpected trials come is to "endure it well." Elder Richard G. Scott taught:

> When you pass through trials for His purposes, as you trust Him, exercise faith in Him, He will help you. That support will generally come step by step, a portion at a time. While you are passing through each phase, the pain and difficulty that comes from being enlarged will continue. If all matters were immediately resolved at your first petition, you could not grow. Your Father in Heaven and His Beloved Son love you perfectly. They would not require you to experience a moment more of difficulty than is absolutely needed for your personal benefit or for that of those you love.[16]

We must respond to our challenges on the basis of our covenants rather than on the basis of our outrage over perceived injustices. It is our covenants that point us toward the Atonement. It is our covenants that help tether us on the path to exaltation. It is our covenants that help us to become like Him—obedient, prayerful, willing to sacrifice and consecrate all, to always remember Him, to be guided by the Spirit, and to remain pure and unspotted from the world. We must always remember to keep our covenants just as He kept His. Because of His pure love for us, "The Son of Man hath descended below them all." And we must ask ourselves, "Art thou greater than he?"[17]

As a marathon runner, I love the Lord's next counsel given to Joseph and to us: "Therefore, hold on thy way, and the priesthood shall remain with thee; for their bounds are set, they cannot pass. Thy days are known, and thy years shall not be numbered less; therefore, fear not what man can do, for God shall be with you forever and ever."[18] I love the message of that scripture—"hold on thy way." "Press forward with a steadfastness in Christ,"[19] relying on the "merits, and mercy, and grace of the Holy Messiah,"[20] and He "shall be with you forever and ever."[21] He has promised each of us, "I will go before your face. I will be on your right hand and on your left, and my Spirit shall be in your hearts, and mine angels round about you, to bear you up."[22]

Because of His love for us, He descended below all things that we would suffer so that He would know how to *succor* us, or in other words, *run to* us in our time of greatest need. And that is exactly what happened to me. It was real and it was tangible, and I knew then and know now that whenever there is something so difficult that I cannot bear it, He will. He will be there to lift that load or burden or pain or infirmity.[23]

As Elder Sterling W. Sill once said, "You were not sent into the vineyard to eat the grapes." The Lord fashioned

37

a testing center that would enable us to demonstrate our love for him by keeping our covenants with Him.[24] There will come times when we may want to cry out like Joseph, "O God, where art thou?" To such a question, there is really only one answer: I am here. I am always here. I will watch over you.

SERVICE

It has been said that adoration of Him must always lead to emulation of Him.[25] President Thomas S. Monson has a beautiful painting of the Savior by the artist Heinrich Hoffman, hanging in his office where he can see it from his desk. He once said, "I have tried to pattern my life after the Master. Whenever I have had a difficult decision to make, I have always looked at that picture and asked myself, 'What would He do?' Then I try to do it."[26]

President Henry B. Eyring teaches that keeping the first commandment naturally leads to keeping the second because to love the Father and the Son is to serve those they love and in that service, our love of God increases and our very nature changes. He said: "In the Master's service, you will come to know and love Him. You will, if you persevere in prayer and faithful service, begin to sense that the Holy Ghost has become a companion. . . . The temptation to do evil seemed to lessen. The desire to do good increased. Those who knew you best and loved you may

---

Left: Heinrich Hoffman, Portrait of Christ, the Savior.
© *by Intellectual Reserve, Inc.*

have said, 'You have become more kind, more patient. You don't seem to be the same person.'"[27]

You wouldn't be the same person because the Atonement of Jesus Christ is real. And the promise is real that we can become new, changed, and better.

A year ago I was released from my calling as the Young Women general president. I loved having the opportunity to serve the Lord with all my heart, might, mind, and strength. I loved my associations with the Brethren, with the young women, and with their magnificent mothers and leaders. I loved teaching and training and testifying of the Savior, of His virtue, of His holy temple, and of His role in the great plan of happiness. I wondered for a long time what I could or should do next. Then one day, as I looked at a painting hanging on the wall of our bedroom of the Savior standing on the shores of the Sea of Galilee, the great question that the Savior asked His Apostles on that shore came into *my* mind: "Lovest thou me?"[28] Elaine, lovest thou me?

As you recall, after the Savior's Crucifixion, His Apostles didn't know what to do. Peter's response was "I go a fishing."[29] In other words, "I guess I will just go back to my old life, my old ways, my previous comfort zone." Several of the other disciples agreed and followed Peter onto a fishing boat to resume the life they had left. That was exactly what I was thinking that morning lying in bed in our home with nowhere to go and nothing to do. "Well," I reasoned, "I will just go back to my old life—see the kids more, maybe even become a pest. Start playing tennis, run more, have great adventures, go back to the book club." But as I looked at that painting hanging in our bedroom, it spoke so personally to me as I recalled that scene in the scriptures when the disciples went back to their "old life." They fished all night and never caught a single fish. And then as morning approached, and they were headed to shore, they saw a distant figure standing on the shore and heard him call to them: "Cast the net on the right side of the ship, and ye shall find,"[30] and they drew "a great multitude of fishes,"[31] enough that their nets broke, and "they were not able to draw it for the multitude of fishes."[32] John recognized who was speaking and said, "It is the Lord."[33] And then we know that Peter went over the edge of the boat and ran to the Savior standing on the shore. I can only imagine the joy of that reunion, but what happened next is the lesson I learned and want to share. Elder Jeffrey R. Holland's words in his general conference talk entitled "The First Great Commandment" say it best. He taught, and I quote:

> After a joyful reunion with the resurrected Jesus, Peter had an exchange with the Savior that I consider the crucial turning point of the apostolic ministry generally and certainly for Peter personally, moving this great rock of a man to a majestic life of devoted service and leadership. Looking at their battered little boats, their frayed nets, and a stunning pile of 153 fish, Jesus said to His senior Apostle, "Peter, do you love me more than you love all this?" Peter said, "Yea, Lord; thou knowest that I love thee."
>
> The Savior responds to that reply but continues to look into the eyes of His disciple and says again, "Peter, do you love me?" Undoubtedly confused a bit by the

41

repetition of the question, the great fisherman answers a second time, "Yea, Lord; thou knowest that I love thee."

The Savior again gives a brief response, but with relentless scrutiny He asks for the third time, "Peter, do you love me?" By now surely Peter is feeling truly uncomfortable . . . Whatever his feelings, Peter said for the third time, "Lord, . . . thou knowest that I love thee."[34] To which Jesus responded . . . perhaps saying something like: "Then Peter, why are you here? Why are we back on this same shore, by these same nets, having this same conversation? Wasn't it obvious then and isn't it obvious now that if I want fish, I can get fish? What I need, Peter, are disciples—and I need them forever. I need someone to feed my sheep and save my lambs. I need someone to preach my gospel and defend my faith. I need someone who loves me, truly, truly loves me, and loves what our Father in Heaven has commissioned me to do. Ours is not a feeble message. It is not a fleeting task. It is not hapless; it is not hopeless; it is not to be consigned to the ash heap of history. It is the work of Almighty God, and it is to change the world."[35]

I testify that this is the work of the Almighty God, and God so loved the world that He sent His Only Begotten Son. And yes, we are here to change the world! As President Eyring once taught: "[We] are called to represent the Savior.

Right: David Lindsley, Feed My Lambs. *© by Intellectual Reserve, Inc.*

[Our] voice to testify becomes the same as His voice, [our] hands to lift the same as His hands. His work is to bless His Father's spirit children with the opportunity to choose eternal life. So, [our] calling is to bless lives."[36] Whether we have a specific calling or not, we can do that. We can be His disciples. We just need to do as the children's song suggests, "Try to be like him, try, try, try."[37] For the crowning characteristic of our love of Him is our loyalty to Him.[38]

I testify that He lives, that He is very near, and that as you and I take what we learn as we serve in callings and continue that service—even after we are seemingly "released"—He will be with us, He will enable us, He will magnify us as His disciples. I also testify that when we fall or feel broken in any way, He will "run to us." He will heal us! He will lift us up!

I am humbled and overwhelmed at the love Jesus offers us, and I testify of His matchless love, which we feel today and can feel always. Love, His pure love, is the power that will change the world!

> I marvel that he would descend from his throne
> divine
> To rescue a soul so rebellious and proud as mine,
> That he should extend his great love unto such as I,
> Sufficient to own, to redeem, and to justify. . . .
> Oh, it is wonderful, wonderful to me.[39]

In the name of Jesus Christ, amen.

NOTES

1. Charles H. Gabriel, "I Stand All Amazed," *Hymns* (Salt Lake City: The Church of Jesus Christ of Latter-day Saints, 1985), no. 193; emphasis added.

2. Gabriel, "I Stand All Amazed."

3. See Jeffrey R. Holland, "I Stand All Amazed," *Ensign*, August 1986, 68–73.

4. Isaiah 6:8.

5. Moroni 7:47; 8:17.

6. See "The Living Christ: The Testimony of the Apostles," *Ensign*, April 2000, 2–3.

7. See "The Living Christ."

8. John 10:30.

9. John 8:29.

10. John 3:16.

11. Samuel Medley, "I Know That My Redeemer Lives," *Hymns*, no. 136.

12. Matthew 11:28–30.

13. Gabriel, "I Stand All Amazed."

14. D&C 121:1–2.

15. D&C 121:7–8.

16. Richard G. Scott, "Trust in the Lord," *Ensign*, November 1995, 17.

17. D&C 122:8.

18. D&C 122:9.

19. 2 Nephi 31:20.

20. 2 Nephi 2:8.

21. D&C 122:9.

22. D&C 84:88.

23. See Alma 7:11.

24. Ted L. Gibbons, *LDS Living*, lesson 28, "Oh God, Where Art Thou?"

25. See Neal A. Maxwell, "In Him All Things Hold Together," *Brigham Young University Speeches* (Provo, UT: University Publications), 103–12.

26. Heidi S. Swinton, *To the Rescue: The Biography of Thomas S. Monson* (Salt Lake City: Deseret Book, 2010), 135.

27. Henry B. Eyring, "In the Strength of the Lord," *Ensign*, May 2004, 19.

28. John 21:15–17.

29. John 21:3.

30. John 21:6.

31. Luke 5:6.

32. John 21:6.

33. John 21:7.

34. See John 21:17.

35. Jeffrey R. Holland, "The First Great Commandment," *Ensign*, November 2012, 84.

36. Henry B. Eyring, "Rise to Your Call," *Ensign*, November 2002, 76.

37. James R. Murray, "Jesus Once Was a Little Child," *Children's Songbook* (Salt Lake City: The Church of Jesus Christ of Latter-day Saints, 1995), 55.

38. See Jeffrey R. Holland, "The First Great Commandment," *Ensign*, November 2012, 83–85.

39. Gabriel, "I Stand All Amazed."

MATTHEW O. RICHARDSON

THE SAVIOR'S LOVE

I n 1966, Aubrey Singer, a producer for the British Broadcasting System, conceived an idea of bringing together creative individuals, artists, and unique events from nineteen different nations to appear on a live global television link. Such an event, at least from a technological standpoint, would hardly draw any attention today. But in 1967, an event like this had never been attempted before. Singer's dream became a reality on June 25, when the largest television audience at that time, estimated to be over 400 million people in twenty-five countries, watched musicians, leaders, artists, and iconic images live via satellite. Even after forty years, the program is still listed as one of the most watched television events in history.

MATTHEW O. RICHARDSON is advancement vice president and a professor of Church history and doctrine at Brigham Young University.

The most memorable event of the broadcast turned out to be a musical number commissioned by the British Broadcasting Corporation for the United Kingdom's contribution. The BBC hoped that a song could be written that everyone could easily understand. They turned to John Lennon and Paul McCartney of the Beatles, who wrote a simple song with the phrases "all you need is love" and "love is all you need" repeated fifty-one times throughout the lyrics. To make the message even easier to understand, they composed a chorus (repeated twice) that chants the word "love" nine times in succession. Brian Epstein, the Beatles' manager at the time, said, "The nice thing about it is that it cannot be misinterpreted."[1]

A recent response to a posting by a student on a popular website asking for help with homework, however, may prove Mr. Epstein's statement wrong. The student posted, "I am doing my homework, and we have to write 10 reasons why love is so misunderstood." Among the many, many answers given, a person responded, "The main reason love is misunderstood is people misunderstand it." While this response doesn't move the needle on the meter for higher critical thinking and reasoning, it does demonstrate that love, even when presented in simple ways, is more often than not misunderstood and misinterpreted.

Such misunderstanding shouldn't be that surprising. After all, the very language we use to create clarity is dependent on our ability to accurately decipher words, understand context, and combine words and meanings appropriately. This is not easy. For example,

Sixties rock band The Beatles wave to fans after arriving at Kennedy Airport in New York, 1964. Members John Lennon (far left) and Paul McCartney (second from left) wrote the song "All You Need Is Love." United Press International, photographer unknown; courtesy of Wikimedia Commons.

it is perfectly acceptable for one person to claim to be "in love" with another. When I was a child, if someone said, "I love Lisa," it was not uncommon for other children to respond, "Then why don't you marry her?" and then giggle to their hearts' delight. But one could use the same word, in the same phrase, but speak about a place, idea, or thing. Thus one might say, "I love ice cream." And others might still respond with, "Then why don't you marry it?" While such a response is absurd, it is technically permissible because of the acceptably loose use of the word. Some may turn to a dictionary to avoid such awkward miscommunications, but they find that the word *love* is defined as an intense feeling, deep affection, a romantic feeling, sexual attraction, or even sexual behavior. The point here is that our language allows for misunderstanding and misinterpretation, making it our responsibility to decipher, contextualize, and apply expressions accurately. We cannot take a word at face value—especially when it comes to the word *love*.

When it comes to understanding the meaning of love, Elder Marvin J. Ashton cautioned, "Too often expediency, infatuation, stimulation, persuasion, or lust are mistaken for love." Sadly, the world may readily embrace these types of misstated ideas and concepts as love, and, as a result, they tend to be disappointed and disillusioned with the outcome. Elder Ashton points out, "How hollow, how empty if our love is no deeper than the arousal of momentary feeling or the expression in words of what is no more lasting than the time it takes to speak them."[2]

> *Love typically spoken of in the world is potentially dangerous not because it is mistaken or bad, but because it most often presents only a part of love's real meaning.*

After saying that the Beatles' new song couldn't be misinterpreted, Mr. Epstein went on to say that the song "is a clear message saying that love is everything."[3] At face value, it is easy to embrace Mr. Epstein's assessment; for intuitively, it sounds right, seems right, and even feels right. In 1969, however, just two years after "All You Need is Love" reached the top of the music charts and during a time when antiwar slogans evoking the name of love were widely used, President Gordon B. Hinckley cautioned that there are those who "clamor for love as the solution to the world's

Gordon B. Hinckley, *photo by Jed A. Clark.*
© *by Intellectual Reserve, Inc.*

problems." He then warned, "Their expression may sound genuine, but their coin is counterfeit. Too often the love of which they speak is at best only hollow mummery."[4] President Hinckley's comments are vital because he was pointing out something very different than love being mistaken for some other feeling, action, or idea. A counterfeit is an imitation or forgery of the real thing, and *mummery* means to mutter, murmur, or act in mime. It is important to consider that muttering, murmuring, and miming are tools used to express something while purposefully holding back full intent or meaning. Thus President Hinckley's insightful description of this type of love being mummery helps us see that the love typically spoken of in the world is potentially dangerous not because it is mistaken or bad, but because it most often presents only a part of love's real meaning. As such, this prohibits us from understanding the authentic nature of love. You see, most uses of the word *love* focus on traits or parts of love but fail to speak about the real thing—the total package. This, as President Hinckley astutely points out, makes love counterfeit and mummery.

With all this in mind, it is imperative to consider the essence of love—in its authentic, genuine form. If we accept a diluted form of love or embrace a counterfeit, we forfeit the full understanding and full rewards predicated upon real love (see D&C 130:20). John emphasizes this very point as he writes, "And these things write we unto you, that your joy may be full" (1 John 1:4). *Full*, in this context, is used to translate the Greek word *pleroo*, meaning "replete, or finished." In some interpretations, *pleroo* is described as a "filler" that rounds out imperfections or dents or makes something complete. This is important to understand, for the love we are speaking of here is a full measure of love and the only means whereby our joy may be made complete or full.

President Hinckley taught that the full essence of love is like the polar star. He said: "In a changing world, it is a constant. It is of the very essence of the gospel. It is the security of the home. It is the safeguard of community life. It is a beacon of hope in a world of distress."[5] When seeking this type of love, we must understand that the night sky is filled with a myriad of unfixed stars—

Harry Anderson, Christ with the Children. © *by Intellectual Reserve, Inc.*

counterfeit polar stars—each fawning for our attention as if it were the sure guiding light. These counterfeits can provide some measure of illumination and guidance, but only one star provides the constant answer for an ever-changing world. The scriptures tell us that the full essence of love "suffereth long, and is kind, and envieth not, and is not puffed up, seeketh not her own, is not easily provoked, thinketh no evil, and rejoiceth not in iniquity but rejoiceth in the truth, beareth all things, believeth all things, hopeth all things, endureth all things" (Moroni 7:45). So important is this authentic form of love that those who are not found possessing it in the last day are "nothing" (Moroni 7:44). Love in its fullest sense is free from the world's dilutions and wickedness and, as President Hinckley described, "savors of the sweet, all-encompassing love of Christ."[6] No wonder Moroni called this love "the pure love of Christ" (Moroni 7:47).

WHAT IS LOVE?

Those who would like to learn about the Savior's love begin with a willingness to consider that the scriptural essence of love might be something very different from what they are either used to hearing or have come to expect. If one approaches learning about the Savior's love with a casual, self-satisfied attitude, only varying portions of the fulness can be realized. This is not to say that we are incapable of loving or that the love of the Savior is beyond our grasp, but merely that truly understanding the love of the Savior is profoundly simple and untainted by humankind's ways. The teachings that help us understand Christ's love are not wrought with distractions or pomp of their own, and therein lies the danger. With such a clean and simple approach to love, even Saints are tempted to spruce it up a bit, add our own agendas, become satisfied with a status quo vision, or allow the views of the world to define our understanding. When properly understood, however, the love of the Savior provides direction for all mankind. The scriptures and prophetic teachings accurately frame the love of God and the Savior.

"GOD IS LOVE"

The scriptures invite us to "love one another" (John 13:35; 15:12; 1 John 3:11, 23; 4:11). Most of us have accepted this invitation at one time or another in our lives and have loved someone (or at least some*thing*). Godly love, however, does not mesh with traditional concepts. The fulness of love is considerably narrow in comparison to the world's concept of love. "Love one another," John wrote, "for love is of God" (1 John 4:7). The scriptures connect the fulness of love not with casual emotions, affection, or even passion, but with God. To ensure that he was not misunderstood, John taught in the simplest of terms that "God is love" (1 John 4:8, 16). This means that if one desires true love, one must understand God.

Some may become nervous using God and Jesus Christ as the standard and definition of love. They may think such a standard is too restrictive or unrealistic. Some may feel that if God defines love, then romance will be replaced with benevolence or brotherly love. But when we understand John's teaching of love correctly, romantic love, brotherly love, and benevolence can be appropriate under God's divine guidance.[7] The Savior's love will, however, exclude feelings, actions, and motives that are contrary to his law. That filters out the misconceptions of love, leaving only a "pure" love (Moroni 7:47). To those who feel that "God is love" is an unrealistic standard, I offer President Henry B. Eyring's advice: "You need not fear that using God as your standard will overwhelm you. On the contrary—God asks only that we approach him humbly, as a child."[8] As we raise our standards to meet those of God and Jesus Christ, we not only begin to act like them but become more like them as well.

"WE LOVE HIM, BECAUSE HE FIRST LOVED US"

Another important consideration in understanding the Savior's love is the statement that "herein is love, not that we loved God, but that he loved us" (1 John 4:10). Although love is intended to eventually become a reciprocal relationship, we must understand that the love of God is not contingent upon our love for him; love begins with God, not with us. John explained that "we love him, because he first loved us" (1 John 4:19). Rather than considering these statements as a reason for us to love God, we can see that John's point is that love begins with God. Thus his love is what allows us to love not only him but everything.

"HE THAT DWELLETH IN LOVE

DWELLETH IN GOD"

The scriptures make it clear that "he that dwelleth in love dwelleth in God, and God in him," (1 John 4:16). Because the love of God is the genesis of our ability to truly love, if we remove God for any reason, we forfeit our ability to practice love in its fullest sense. For example, John taught that "if any man love the world, the love of the Father is not in him" (1 John 2:15). This is not to say that if one indulges in worldliness God will no longer love him or her. C. S. Lewis emphasized that "the great thing to remember is that, though our feelings come and go, His [God's] love for us does not. It is not wearied by our sins, or our indifference."[9]

Although God will always love us, John emphasized that our love of the world limits the degree to which God's Spirit is manifest in our lives. How we embrace the world, whether with unabashed acceptance or with flirtatious encounters with its subtleties, creates a boundary between God and us. James, author of the Epistle of James, queried, "Know ye not that the friendship of the world is enmity with God?" He concluded, "Whosoever therefore will be a friend of the world is the enemy of God" (James 4:4). When we entertain that which removes God from our lives, it is not his love for us that decreases but the presence of his Spirit that diminishes (see D&C 121:37). Although God still loves us, our understanding and ability to truly love is forfeited because of the loss of his Spirit. Where God is not, love in its fulness cannot be. This forfeiture is not restricted to wicked acts alone but can include using the world to define gospel principles.

With the connection between love and God established, we can turn our focus to John's teachings about "the love of God" (1 John 3:16). When discussing God the Father's love for us, the scriptures once again provide critical commentary: "For God so loved the world, that he gave his only begotten Son" (John 3:16). Here John links God's love for the world with Jesus Christ. Later, John writes, "In this was manifested the love of God toward us, because that God sent his only begotten Son into the world, that we might live through him" (1 John 4:9). According to John, the love of God manifest to us is Jesus Christ.

An earlier witness of this concept is found in the Book of Mormon. Young Nephi saw a tree, "and the beauty thereof was far beyond, yea, exceeding of all beauty; and the whiteness thereof did exceed the whiteness of the driven snow" (1 Nephi 11:8). When Nephi asked for an interpretation of what the tree is, rather than giving an immediate answer, a vision of the birth of Jesus Christ was opened to him (see 1 Nephi 11:13–20). As the vision closed, the angel proclaimed, "Behold the Lamb of God, yea, even the Son of the Eternal Father!" The angel then asked Nephi, "Knowest thou the meaning of the

Right: Jerry Thompson, **Lehi's Dream.** *© by Intellectual Reserve, Inc.*

tree which thy father saw?" (1 Nephi 11:21). The angel seems to have been checking to see if Nephi grasped the relationship between the vision of the Savior and his inquiry concerning the interpretation of the tree. Immediately, Nephi astutely answered, "Yea, it [the tree] is the love of God, which sheddeth itself abroad in the hearts of the children of men; wherefore, it is the most desirable above all things" (1 Nephi 11:22). Both Nephi and John testified that Jesus Christ is the love of God made manifest to us.

THE FATHER GAVE ALL THINGS TO THE SON

Although Christ emphasized "my Father is greater than I" (John 14:28), he did not diminish his authoritative role in manifesting the Father's love. John recorded Christ's words as "Father, I will that they also, whom thou hast given me, be with me where I am; that they may behold my glory, which thou hast given me: for thou lovedst me before the foundation of the world" (John 17:24). Christ's glory was given to him by God because of his Father's love. John further testified that "the Father loveth the Son, and hath given all things into his hand" (John 3:35). It was through God's love that Christ became the chosen and authoritative manifestation of the Father. John said of Christ's ministry that "the Father loveth the Son, and sheweth him all things that himself doeth: and he will shew him greater works than these, that ye may marvel" (John 5:20). Christ, commissioned of the Father, manifests the fulness of the Father to all mankind. Thus Christ is a mediator or a propitiator (see 1 John 4:10). Though a mediator and a propitiator are similar, Richard D. Draper explains that propitiation goes beyond mediation by uniting two parties in friendship.[10] It is Christ, therefore, who makes it possible for us to receive the fulness of God's love. John emphasized this relationship as he taught, "I am the way, the truth, and the life: no man cometh unto the Father, but by me" (John 14:6).

"BORN OF GOD"

If we expect to obtain the fulness of God's love, we must receive it through the propitiation of Jesus Christ. We are reminded that "love is of God; and every one that loveth is born of God, and knoweth God" (1 John 4:7). To receive and exercise God's love requires us to be "born of God." To some, being born of God is receiving the realization that God is our spiritual Father and that we are his spiritual offspring. To others, being born of God involves recognizing that Jesus Christ is our Savior. It is clear that being "born of God," as spoken in this passage, is more than just realizing that our beginnings were with God the Father or proclaiming that Jesus Christ is our personal Savior.

As Jesus taught Nicodemus, he emphasized that one must be "born again" to see the kingdom of God

It is clear that being "born of God" . . . is more than just realizing that our beginnings were with God the Father or proclaiming that Jesus Christ is our personal Savior.

(John 3:3). The Prophet Joseph Smith further clarified that we "must have a change of heart to see the kingdom of God."[11] It was later emphasized that our ability to love ("everyone that loveth") is born of God. It is true that our ability to love stems from God, but how is the love of God born in us? We may also ponder how love relates to changing our hearts and becoming born again. Elder Bruce R. McConkie wrote, "To be born does not mean to come into existence out of nothing, but rather to begin a new type of existence, to live again in a changed situation. Birth is the continuation of life under different circumstances."[12] Thus, "whosoever believeth that Jesus is the Christ is born of God" (1 John 5:1) or, in other words, must begin a renovation. We can no longer remain the same people we once were. Those who embrace the gospel of Christ become new creatures, born into new situations, new circumstances, new expectations, a new way to approach daily experiences, and a new way to love. When we believe in Christ, we begin a new existence, a life with Christ and of Christ. Those who were unable to love in the past can be transformed and find love born in them. This type of transformation is accomplished only through the love of Jesus Christ.

"CALLED THE SONS OF GOD"

It is interesting that the scriptures link the love of God with not only a symbolic rebirth but a metaphorical adoption as well. John taught that the love of God necessarily leads to both a rebirth and an adoption.

"Behold, what manner of love the Father hath bestowed upon us," John wrote, "that we should be called the sons of God" (1 John 3:1). This verse possesses a flavor of wonderment that God's love is so grand that mere men can be called the sons of God. To some it may seem odd that John wrote of this event with wonder. John understood that we were created by God, thus becoming, as God's creations, his sons and daughters. But John stated that God's love was bestowed upon us so that we *should* be called sons of God.

Other prophets testify of this relationship between love, rebirth, and becoming the children of God. The prophet Moroni was emphatic about obtaining the love of God and thus becoming sons of God. He pleaded with those who would hear his message to "pray unto the Father with all the energy of heart, that ye may be filled with this love [the love of Christ, or charity], which he hath bestowed upon all who are true followers of his Son, Jesus Christ; that ye may become the sons of God" (Moroni 7:48).

Another prophet, King Benjamin, addressed the importance of understanding this adoptive process. He explained that "because of the covenant which ye have made ye shall be called the children of Christ, his sons, and his daughters; for behold, this day he hath spiritually begotten you; for ye say that your hearts are changed through faith on his name; therefore, ye are born of him and have become his sons and his daughters. And under this head ye are made free, and there is no other head whereby ye can be made free" (Mosiah 5:7–8). Benjamin testified that this adoption was made possible because of the covenant we made with God.

This adoptive process is an essential part of the rebirth. Again we return to Christ's discourse to Nicodemus. After teaching of the necessity of the rebirth of the heart, Christ told Nicodemus, "Verily, verily, I say unto thee, Except a man be born of water and of the Spirit, he cannot enter into the kingdom of God" (John 3:5). He summarized, "Marvel not that I said unto thee, Ye must be born again" (John 3:7). The Prophet Joseph Smith, when referring to these passages, taught that we must "subscribe [to] the articles of adoption to enter therein."[13] The process of being born again requires more than acknowledging Christ and his mission. It requires even more than a change of heart. It requires subscribing to the articles of adoption—making covenants. Elder Bruce R. McConkie stated that the sons and daughters of Jesus Christ "take upon them his name in the waters of baptism and certify anew each time they partake of the sacrament that they have so done; or, more accurately, in the waters of baptism power is given them to become sons of Christ, which eventuates when they are in fact born of Spirit and become new creatures of the Holy Ghost."[14] Because the love of God is manifest through Christ, we can know God only through Christ. We can experience the fulness of God's love only by entering into a covenant relationship with Jesus Christ.

Right: Harry Anderson, Jesus Christ. *© by Intellectual Reserve, Inc.*

By maintaining our covenantal status, we are born of God and thus become the sons and daughters of Christ.

Whether the discussion is about becoming reborn or becoming children of God, Christ is always at the center of the discussion. As we receive Christ and exercise the power given us by him, we become his sons and daughters (see John 1:12). Elder McConkie further clarified the connection between rebirth/adoption and Jesus Christ when he explained: "Those accountable mortals who then believe and obey the gospel are born again; they are born of the Spirit; they become alive to the things of righteousness or of the Spirit. They become members of another family; have new brothers and sisters, and a new Father. They are the sons and daughters of Jesus Christ."[15]

Because the love of God is manifest through Christ, we can know God only through Christ.

Although this adoption is necessary, it is not a culminating event but a part of a continual process of change. That is apparent in John's writing: "Beloved, now are we the sons of God, and it doth not yet appear what we shall be: but we know that, when he shall appear, we shall be like him; for we shall see him as he is" (1 John 3:2). The process of receiving God's and the Savior's love, rebirth, and becoming the children of Christ is not a one-time event but a gradual experience. In this process, we shall become like Christ (see 1 John 3:2).

"If Ye Love Me, Keep My Commandments"

As sons and daughters of Christ, we have covenanted to keep his commandments. Jesus taught, "If ye love me, keep my commandments" (John 14:15). This implies that we will keep the commandments because we love Christ (see 1 John 5:2–3; 2 John 1:6). Though this is true, an additional aspect of obedience is presented in John's writings. Christ taught that "he that hath my commandments, and keepeth them, he it is that loveth me: and he that loveth me shall be loved of my Father, and I will love him, and will manifest myself to him" (John 14:21). When we keep the commandments, we find that Christ manifests himself to us.

This simple concept presents an interesting situation. Many of those who keep the commandments do so because they already possess a love of Christ. They, according to the prophetic blessing, will have a manifestation of Christ. But consider these verses applied in other circumstances. What of those who have not yet come to love Christ? Are they to be obedient to God's commandments as well? C. S. Lewis felt that some people worry because they are unsure if they love God. He said concerning these people: "They are told they ought to love God. They cannot find any such feelings in themselves. What are they to do? . . . Act as if you did. Do not sit trying to manufacture feelings. Ask yourself, 'If I were sure that I loved God, what would I do?' When you have found the answer, go and do it."[16] Lewis further observed: "As soon as we do this we find one of the great secrets. When you are behaving as if you loved someone, you will presently come to love him,"[17] Jesus himself taught that "if any man will do his [God's] will, he shall know of the doctrine, whether it be of God, or whether I speak of myself" (John 7:17). Not only will the obedient know the divine source of the doctrine, but they will grow in love toward the Master as well. Thus the cycle of love and obedience begins anew, ever deepening with each act of obedience and receipt of divine manifestation.

Our obedience maintains our covenant relationship with Christ, which facilitates the manifestation of God's love. We can feel the fulness of the Father only when our covenants with Christ are in effect. As we become more proficient in maintaining our covenant of keeping the commandments, not only do we draw ever closer to the Savior but he becomes a constant fixture in our lives. Christ taught, "If a man love me, he will keep my words: and my Father will love him, and we will come unto him, and make our abode with him" (John 14:23).

"LOVE ONE ANOTHER; AS I HAVE LOVED YOU"

Disciples of Christ are reminded that mere familiarity with the Savior's message is not sufficient to obtain the full love of God. "My little children," John counseled, "let us not love in word, neither in tongue; but in deed and in truth" (1 John 3:18). President Howard W. Hunter taught: "Merely saying, accepting, believing are

not enough. They are incomplete until that which they imply is translated into the dynamic action of daily living."[18] A disciple of Christ, therefore, is one who not only receives Christ's law but also seeks to follow the given counsel (see D&C 41:5). In the same manner, we find that a disciple of Christ is not only one who receives God's love and who loves God but one who seeks to love others. Christ commanded "that he who loveth God love his brother also" (1 John 4:21). This commandment was at the heart of Christ's ministry from the beginning (see 1 John 3:11; John 15:17).

Loving others is regarded as the badge of Christianity. Christ taught that "by their fruits ye shall know them" (Matthew 7:20). The discerning fruit of discipleship was determined by whether the followers of Christ loved others; "By this shall all men know that ye are my disciples," Christ taught, "if ye have love one to another" (John 13:35).

Although we have covenanted to love others, it is not enough to merely go through the motions in hopes of checking off one more requirement of discipleship. It is true that Christ admonished us to "love one another." But his commandment was not merely to learn to love others but to "love one another; as I have loved you, that ye also love one another" (John 13:34; see also John 15:12; 1 John 3:23). This pattern was familiar to Christ, for he taught that "as the Father hath loved me, so have I loved you: continue ye in my love" (John 15:9). No wonder John, who was self-described as "the disciple whom Jesus loved,"[19] wrote so much concerning loving others. Since

John received Christ's love, he was in a position to love others; and he understood that he must continue in that love by loving others as Christ loved him. Elder C. Max Caldwell said, "Jesus' love was inseparably connected to and resulted from his life of serving, sacrificing, and giving in behalf of others. We cannot develop Christlike love except by practicing the process prescribed by the Master."[20]

"GREATER LOVE HATH NO MAN"[21]

As we consider the depth of the love that is God's to give, it is really quite amazing to think that it has been made available to us. The pinnacle of our understanding of the love of God is centered not only upon Christ, but also upon his sacrifice (see 1 John 4:9). The scriptures teach that we "perceive . . . the love of God, because he laid down his life for us" (1 John 3:16) and that the love of God is manifested toward us, *because* "God sent his only begotten Son into the world, [so] that we might live through him" (1 John 4:9). Paul taught that "if any man live in Christ, he is a new creature: old things are passed away; behold, all things are become new" (Joseph Smith Translation, 2 Corinthians 5:17).[22] The Savior's mission—his sacrifice—in some miraculous way changes not only how we live and love but also

> *"At that ultimate stage [eternal life] we will exhibit divine characteristics not just because we think we should but because that is the way we are."*

changes us. "The Atonement in some way," wrote Elder Bruce C. Hafen, "apparently through the Holy Ghost, makes possible the infusion of spiritual endowments that actually change and purify our nature, moving us toward that state of holiness or completeness we call eternal life or Godlike life. At that ultimate stage we will exhibit divine characteristics not just because we think we should but because that is the way we are."[23] It is through this change that we can find everlasting life. John reminded us that "God so loved the world, that he gave his only begotten Son, that whosoever believeth in him should not perish, but have everlasting life" (John 3:16). Jesus Christ, the love of God, provides hope of salvation. No wonder John exults, "There is no fear in love; but perfect love casteth out fear: because fear hath torment. He that feareth is not made perfect in love" (1 John 4:18).

"THE FULNESS"

"What manner of love the Father hath bestowed upon us" (1 John 3:1)? The scriptures clearly teach of a fulness of love: not a counterfeit love, nor a portion of love, but a fulness thereof. We begin to understand that the full measure of love is founded in God. It is from God that all love springs forth. We learn that Jesus Christ is, in reality, the love of God, and thus we can feel of the fulness of God's love as we enter into a covenant and become born of Christ. We reciprocate the Savior's love by keeping the commandments and loving others. It is because of the ultimate sacrifice, the fulfilling of the mission of Christ, that we are able to become new creatures and thereby love others as Christ loved us. This is the only way to find the love that will guide and direct our lives for peace, dispose of fear, and bring us to a fulness of joy: to be filled with pure love—even Jesus Christ.

Thus, to a world that clamors for love as the solution to the world's problems and sings that love—in any form—is all we need, here are the lyrics to yet one more song:

> I feel my Savior's love
> In all the world around me.
> His Spirit warms my soul
> Through ev'rything I see.
>
> I feel my Savior's love;
> Its gentleness enfolds me,
> And when I kneel to pray,
> My heart is filled with peace.
>
> I feel my Savior's love
> And know that he will bless me.
> I offer him my heart;
> My shepherd he will be.
>
> I'll share my Savior's love
> By serving others freely.
> In serving I am blessed.
> In giving I receive.
>
> He knows I will follow him,
> Give all my life to him.

I feel my Savior's love,
The love he freely gives me.[24]

With all this in mind, we can say with assurance that all we need *is* love—the Savior's love.

NOTES

1. Jade Wright, "Rock of Ages," *BNET*, November 27, 2009.

2. Marvin J. Ashton, "Love Takes Time," *Ensign*, November 1975, 108.

3. Wright, "Rock of Ages."

4. Gordon B. Hinckley, in Conference Report, April 1969, 61.

5. Gordon B. Hinckley, "Let Love Be the Lodestar of Your Life," *Ensign*, May 1989, 66.

6. Hinckley, "Lodestar of Your Life," 67.

7. Dr. Richard D. Draper, associate dean of Religious Education at Brigham Young University, concludes that all of the forms of love (*agape*, *philos*, and *eros*), when used appropriately, are necessary to achieve the highest or noblest love (see "Love and Joy," unpublished manuscript).

8. Henry B. Eyring, *To Draw Closer to God* (Salt Lake City: Deseret Book, 1997), 68.

9. C. S. Lewis, *Mere Christianity* (New York: Macmillan, 1952), 102–3.

10. Draper, "Love and Joy," unpublished manuscript.

11. Andrew F. Ehat and Lyndon W. Cook, comps., *The Words of Joseph Smith* (Provo, UT: Religious Studies Center, 1980), 256.

12. McConkie, *Doctrinal New Testament Commentary*, 2:471.

13. Ehat and Cook, *Words of Joseph Smith*, 256.

14. McConkie, *Doctrinal New Testament Commentary*, 2:471–72.

15. McConkie, *Doctrinal New Testament Commentary*, 2:471.

16. Lewis, *Mere Christianity*, 102.

17. Lewis, *Mere Christianity*, 101.

18. Howard W. Hunter, in Conference Report, October 1967, 116.

19. John 21:20; see also John 13:23; 19:26; 20:2; 21:7.

20. C. Max Caldwell, in Conference Report, October 1992, 40.

21. John 15:13.

22. See *The Holy Scriptures: Inspired Version* (Independence, MO: Herald Publishing House, 1991).

23. Bruce C. Hafen, *The Broken Heart* (Salt Lake City: Deseret Book, 1989), 18.

24. Ralph Rodgers Jr., K. Newell Dayley, and Laurie Huffman, "I Feel My Savior's Love," *Children's Songbook* (Salt Lake City: The Church of Jesus Christ of Latter-day Saints, 1989), 74–75.

D. KELLY OGDEN

OUR SAVIOR'S LOVE
MANIFEST IN RESURRECTION

Nothing has ever happened in this world, or any other world of which we know, that compares in grandeur and scope with the events between the Garden of Gethsemane and the Garden of the Resurrection—events that affect the mortal and immortal life of every soul to come into this world.

President Howard W. Hunter proclaimed that "the doctrine of the Resurrection is the single most fundamental and crucial doctrine in the Christian religion. It cannot be overemphasized, nor can it be disregarded. Without the Resurrection, the gospel of Jesus Christ becomes a litany of wise sayings and seemingly unexplainable miracles—but sayings and miracles with no ultimate triumph. No, the ultimate triumph is in the

D. KELLY OGDEN is a professor of ancient scripture at Brigham Young University.

ultimate miracle: for the first time in the history of mankind, one who was dead raised himself into living immortality."[1]

Thanks to Jesus, who died and raised his body to immortality, we can die and be raised to live forever also. One of our colleagues at Brigham Young University had a daughter who died at age thirteen. When she was seven, already struggling with the disease that would eventually take her life, she stood one day in a meeting to bear witness to these beautiful truths: "I love Jesus Christ. Because of him, I only have to die once. I'll never have to die again."

The story of Jesus is not a "womb to tomb" story. As Elder Orson F. Whitney taught, "[His] Death on Calvary was no more the ending, than the Birth in Bethlehem was the beginning, of that Divine Career."[2]

Many Bible scholars recognize the pivotal importance and the far-reaching consequences of the Resurrection of the Lord Jesus Christ. "Were it not for the resurrection event," wrote F. F. Bruce, "there would have been no resurrection faith."[3] The followers of Jesus would not live and die for a lie. Something dramatic and true had changed their lives forever. The fact is, none of the early leaders and preachers in the first-century church could say enough about the Resurrection. It was on the lips of Peter, Stephen, Paul, and all others, everywhere they went and with everyone they taught.

Another prominent scholar declared:

Whether we are comfortable with it or not, Christianity does indeed stand or fall on certain historical facts—not merely historical claims, but historical facts. Among these facts that are most crucial to Christian faith is that of Jesus' resurrection from the dead. The Christian faith is not mere faith in faith . . . but rather, a belief about the significance of certain historical events.[4]

We have to ask, Why is there no other first-century Jew who has millions of followers today? Why isn't there a John the Baptist movement? Why, of all first-century figures, including the Roman emperors, is Jesus still worshiped today, while the others have crumbled into the dust of history?

It's because this Jesus—the historical Jesus—is also the living Lord. That's why. It's because he's still around, while the others are long gone.[5]

The Resurrection literally changed the lives of the early Christians and the lives of all true Christians since that day. The day following the Crucifixion and burial of Jesus was the holy Sabbath, the day the Saints met to worship. But that particular Saturday must have been a Saturday of deepest depression. Who would have wanted to hold a meeting? And who would have been willing to give a talk? What would they have even talked about? It must have been a most oppressive time for the spirits of those early members of the church. But that depressing day was followed, the very next morning, by a Sunday of most brilliant joy.

This single historical fact and doctrine forever changed the course of the ancient Church and the course of the world.

This single historical fact and doctrine forever changed the course of the ancient Church and the course of the world. There is no fact in history that is so widely attested and confirmed by credible witnesses.

WOMEN AND ANGELS: FIRST AT JESUS' TOMB

"In the end of the Sabbath, as it began to dawn toward the first day of the week" (Matthew 28:1), women disciples were making their way toward the tomb when an aftershock of the earthquake of the previous Friday struck Jerusalem again, as angels came down from heaven to open the tomb of God's Son. No heavy stone seal nor secure guard of the Sanhedrin would stand up to nature's convulsive powers directed by the God of the universe, nor could they withstand angelic messengers sent by that very God to open the tomb, revealing Jesus' absence. Jesus' mortal life was terminated at the hands of men, but his postmortal life, again in the mortal sphere, commenced at the hands of the Father and his messengers. The two angels (see Joseph Smith Translation, Matthew 28:2) removed the stone at the entrance of the sepulchre and sat on it (see Joseph Smith Translation, John 20:1).

Jesus did not need angels to roll away the great stone from the door of the sepulchre so that he could leave. Resurrected beings have more refined bodies and have power to pass through the elements and objects of the earth. In the resurrection we shall become acquainted with a whole new dimension of the laws of physics. Why, then, did the angels roll the stone away and open the tomb? First, there was undoubtedly important symbolic meaning in this act. Just as the door of the tomb was now open, signaling its occupant was no longer there, so too the door of the spirit world was now open, signaling that its righteous inhabitants were free from the bondage of death and would no longer be confined there.

First-century tomb near Jerusalem. Courtesy of D. Kelly Ogden.

Second, with the opening of the tomb, the disciples could look inside as well as enter and know for themselves that the tomb was empty, that Jesus had returned to life, that he really was the Savior, with power to raise his own physical body back to life.

Others would likewise come to the tomb, and out of their initial experience with its emptiness would eventually blossom the witness that Jesus was who he said he was, that he had told the truth, that he was the Savior, Messiah, and Son of God, alive again.

Among the women who approached the tomb that glorious morning were Mary Magdalene; Mary, the mother of James the Younger and Joses (Joseph); Salome, the mother of Apostles James and John; and Joanna, wife of Chuza, steward of Herod Antipas (see Luke 8:3; 24:10).We also cannot help but wonder whether the two beloved sisters from Bethany, Martha and Mary, along with some of the Apostles' wives, were also present.

Among the women disciples who followed Jesus, Mary Magdalene seems to have served in a leadership capacity. She is mentioned first in several listings of female followers (see, for example, Matthew 27:56; Luke 24:10), and she was first to see the resurrected Lord (see John 20:1–18). Mary of Magdala appears to have had a preeminent relationship with Jesus of Nazareth.

TESTIMONY OF ANGELS: "HE IS RISEN"

Angelic visitors came at the Savior's birth, during his ministry (for example, at the Transfiguration), in Gethsemane, and now at his tomb. There was frequent contact between heaven and earth while the great Creator sojourned here for a brief time (see Matthew 1:20; 2:13, 19; 4:11; 28:2–8; Luke 1:11–20, 26–30; 2:9–15; 22:43).

When the angels appeared, the guards were scared to death (see Matthew 28:4), but the heavenly messengers calmed the fears of the women, assuring them that the man they were seeking was "not here: for he is risen, as he said" (28:6).

Seeing and hearing astonishing things, Mary Magdalene ran to tell Peter and John (we are not told where James was). Representing all the women, Mary exclaimed to the two leading Apostles: "They have taken away the Lord out of the sepulchre, and we know not where they have laid

Portrayal of Mary Magdalene at the Savior's tomb. Courtesy of D. Kelly Ogden.

him" (John 20:2). If, by mentioning "they" who took away the body, Mary meant the Romans, the Jewish leaders, or even the angels, we cannot be sure. We do however know that she had not quite comprehended the divine message she had heard from those angels: "He is risen; he is not here." It would yet require some personal experience, seeing, hearing, and touching for Mary and for all others to comprehend the glorious fact of resurrection.

They were experiencing, understandably, a dramatic mix of feelings—fright, perplexity, amazement, respect, excitement, joy—over what was happening, and their minds were beginning from these very moments to piece together the doctrines that Jesus had taught that only now, as they actually occurred, could be fully comprehended by mortals.

PETER AND JOHN AT THE TOMB

Years later, Luke, who likely learned what happened next from Peter and John, recorded that the two Apostles, hearing these extraordinary, unbelievable reports, ran together to the sepulchre, John outrunning Peter.

John arrived, stooped down, looked in, and then Peter arrived and immediately entered. Respectfully giving way to the chief Apostle, John waited and then followed Peter inside. They both saw the burial cloths lying where Jesus' body had been. According to his own written report, John "saw, and believed" (John 20:8) that a dead mortal being was alive again. They sensed that there was something very different about this Being. He was not just brought back to life temporarily to eventually die again. Raising of the dead was a miracle they knew not only from scripture but from personal experience, watching Jesus do it at least three times.[6] This was different. The Apostles were coming to understand that their Savior had been raised by the power of the Father into immortality. As the next verse

(John 20:9) explains, up to this point "they knew [or comprehended] not the scripture, that he must rise again from the dead."

We raise the question: how *could* they comprehend such a thing? For four thousand years, mortals had been dying and were buried away, their physical bodies remaining dead, having no spirit, no life. Resurrection had never happened in this world. But now the Apostles were fitting together the current facts and the teachings and the prophecies. They had weighty matters to reflect on.

It seems significant that there are no scriptural records that discuss the details of the actual Resurrection process, or what went on inside the tomb immediately after the Resurrection. We do not know how long Jesus was there. We *do* know that Jesus passed through his burial clothes, leaving them lying in place, in the outline and form of the body around which they had been wrapped. Resurrected bodies have the power to move through solid objects. John recorded in his own Gospel that when he came to the tomb and looked inside, and when Peter entered it shortly thereafter, they both saw the strips of burial linen lying in place in the burial chamber as well as the burial cloth that had been wrapped around Jesus' head (see John 20:4–7). The strips of cloth "were left in such a way as to show that his resurrected body had passed through their folds and strands without the need of unwinding the strips or untying the napkin."[7]

This was explicit evidence of Jesus' Resurrection. No mortal man had disturbed his body. The cloth ("napkin" in the King James Version) that had been wrapped about Jesus' head was still by itself, separate from the linen.

Jesus, then, left his burial cloths in place as another witness of one of the greatest of the miraculous acts that compose the Atonement and Resurrection.

MARY ALONE WITH THE RESURRECTED JESUS

One woman, alone, remained at the sepulchre, crying (see John 20:11–17). Of all the Marys who had been attending to the body, the one from Magdala stooped down and looked into the burial chamber, and saw two angels arrayed in brilliant white "sitting, the one at the head, and the other at the feet, where the body of Jesus had lain."

The angels asked: "Woman, why weepest thou?"

Mary responded: "Because they have taken away my Lord, and I know not where they have laid him."

Mary turned around and saw Jesus, but through her tears she did not recognize him, and when asked who she was looking for, she replied to that man she supposed was the gardener:

"Sir, if thou have borne him hence, tell me where thou hast laid him, and I will take him away."

Jesus spoke her name: "Mary."

Then she recognized him, saying, "Rabboni!" (Master!)

Mary instantly desired to embrace him, but his first embrace was reserved for his Father, then for mortals.

"Hold me not," he gently explained to her, "for I am not yet ascended to my Father: but go to my brethren, and say unto them, I ascend unto my Father, and your Father;

Left: Walter Rane, Mary at Jesus' Tomb. © *by Intellectual Reserve, Inc.*

and to my God, and your God" (Joseph Smith Translation, John 20:17).

There would now be a respectful separation between immortals and mortals. Jesus taught that God was first his Father and God, then our Father and God. And Jesus himself was now more than mortal friend and associate in the divine work—he was Savior, Lord, and God to those men and women and to all humankind.

If, as the Savior indicated, he had not yet ascended to his Father, where had he been? The answer is more gloriously and plainly presented in section 138 of the Doctrine and Covenants than anywhere else in sacred writ. The Lord Jesus Christ had not yet ascended far into space, to the home of his Father, but had gone to the spirit world— which is the dimension of all spirit beings and living things occupying the very same space as this physical earth. He organized in the world of spirits, among the billions of the Father's children who had lived from the days of Adam and Eve until his own day, that same missionary effort that he had organized on earth during his mortal ministry. "And there he preached to them the everlasting gospel, the doctrine of the resurrection and the redemption of mankind from the fall, and from individual sins on condition of repentance" (D&C 138:19).

The great monster death has no more effect on us. As Abinadi said, "There is a resurrection, therefore the grave hath no victory, and the sting of death is swallowed up in Christ" (Mosiah 16:8). In the end, only death will die. All living things (things with spirits) will live forever.

Why is the resurrection of the body so important to each of us? The Prophet Joseph Smith taught: "We came to this earth that we might have a body and present it pure before God in the celestial kingdom. The great principle of happiness consists in having a body."[8] Robert J. Matthews adds: "The resurrection of our individual bodies is important because our Heavenly Father has a resurrected body of flesh and bone (see D&C 130:22). . . . It would be possible to continue in eternity as spirit bodies without the physical body, but as such we could not reach the fulness of salvation. A spirit body without a resurrected physical body cannot obtain a fulness of joy (see D&C 93:33–34)."[9]

OTHER WOMEN ENCOUNTER THE RESURRECTED JESUS

The elect women, chosen to be the first to see the miracle of the Savior's Resurrection, rushed to tell the Apostles that they had personally met and talked with him, had touched his feet (the same feet showing the wounds of crucifixion), and had worshipped him (see Matthew 28:9–10).

"One may wonder," Elder James E. Talmage wrote, "why Jesus had forbidden Mary Magdalene to touch Him, and then, so soon after, had permitted other women to hold Him by the feet as they bowed in reverence. We may assume that Mary's emotional approach had been prompted more by a feeling of personal yet holy affection than by an impulse of devotional worship such as the other women evinced. Though the Resurrected Christ manifested the same friendly and intimate regard as He had shown in the mortal state toward those with whom He had been closely associated, He was no longer one of them in the literal

sense. There was about Him a divine dignity that forbade close personal familiarity."[10]

JESUS APPEARS TO TWO DISCIPLES ON THE ROAD TO EMMAUS

Only Luke narrates a post-Resurrection appearance of Jesus to two disciples walking along the road from Jerusalem down to Emmaus (see Luke 24:13–32). Why would the two disciples not have recognized Jesus right from the beginning of their walk together? They would have been quite familiar with his appearance, his mannerisms, and his way of teaching. Mark notes that "he appeared in another form" (Mark 16:12). As a resurrected being Jesus was certainly in "another form," a condition with which no one on earth (except the women that morning) was yet acquainted. Besides that, Luke points out that "their eyes were holden that they should not know him" (Luke 24:16), the recognition being withheld for a time so that the resurrected Lord could teach them and help them come to an understanding.

"Ought not Christ to have suffered these things, and to enter into his glory?" (Luke 24:26). Was it so difficult to comprehend that Jesus' crown of thorns had to come before his crown of glory? The prophets—the Messiah's forerunners—plainly testified over the course of four millennia that the Messiah (who would eventually rule and

---

Left: Liz Lemon Swindle, On the Road to Emmaus.

reign at his Second Coming to earth) would come at first to suffer, bleed, and die.

As they approached Emmaus, it looked as though Jesus would continue on the road, but the disciples pled with him, since it was getting late in the afternoon, to come in and eat with them. As they were eating, Jesus took some unleavened bread and broke it, blessed it, and handed them some. Their spiritual eyes were opened; they realized who he was, and he disappeared in that instant, leaving them reflecting on the singularity of their feelings: "Did not our heart burn within us, while he talked with us by the way, and while he opened to us the scriptures?" (Luke 24:32). Cleopas and his companion rushed back up to Jerusalem to report to ten Apostles.

> *Luke points out that "their eyes were holden that they should not know him"* . . . *so that the resurrected Lord could teach them.*

JESUS APPEARS TO HIS APOSTLES

Jesus suddenly appeared in the room where they were gathered (not coming in through the door, showing that physical walls are no obstacle for a resurrected being). The Savior greeted them with *shalom aleichem*, Hebrew/ Aramaic for "peace be unto you."

The disciples were startled and afraid, supposing that some spirit had joined them, but Jesus calmed their anxiety and satisfied their curiosity by inviting them to come forth and get acquainted with a resurrected body: "Behold my hands and my feet, that it is I myself: handle me, and see; for a spirit hath not flesh and bones, as ye see me have" (Luke 24:39). He extended his hands and his feet for them to touch, just as he would do for his disciples in the western world: "come forth unto me, that ye may thrust your hands into my side, and also that ye may feel the prints of the nails in my hands and in my feet" (3 Nephi 11:14).

The Lord wanted his still-mortal friends to know that a resurrected, immortal body is very corporeal; the flesh is real and physical—though now in a more refined and perfected condition. It was important for them to see and feel, to be eyewitnesses with an unequivocal testimony of the corporeal nature of the resurrected Lord's body, because for many generations thereafter—from ancient through modern times—some would corrupt and distort the reality of physical resurrection and question the corporeality of Jesus' postmortal body.

The physicality of Jesus' resurrected body pointedly refutes the traditional Christian teaching that Jesus is a mere spiritual essence or influence without a body. If Jesus now has no body, what did he do with his resurrected body? The notion that he is merely a spiritual essence was not taught by him but added later by men.

The disciples were so happy they could hardly believe what was happening, and they continued marveling, trying to figure out how a resurrected body works.

Thomas later desired the same privilege that the other Apostles and the women had received; and an eyewitness he too had to be.

The resurrected Jesus appeared to his Apostles at the Sea of Galilee and further instructed them about resurrection.

Mount Arbel overlooks the Sea of Galilee. Courtesy of D. Kelly Ogden.

Another post-Resurrection appearance of Jesus may have occurred on Mount Arbel, a high point overlooking the whole Sea of Galilee region. There, on the secluded edge of the twelve-hundred-foot precipice, Jesus could have inspired his leading disciples with their commission to take the gospel to all the world (see Matthew 28:16–20; Mark 16:15–18).

When Jesus' Apostles saw him, they worshipped him, Matthew reported (28:17), "but some doubted," otherwise meaning that some *hesitated*; they were still piecing together this wonderful mystery of the resurrected Lord.

Back in the southern part of the land, Jesus led his closest followers out as far as to Bethany (see Luke 24:50), on the eastern slope of the Mount of Olives (see Acts 1:9–12), and there he blessed them.

OTHER APPEARANCES
OF THE RESURRECTED JESUS

The scriptures go on to relate the visits of the risen Lord with members of the Twelve in Galilee (see John 21), with more than five hundred brethren (noted in 1 Corinthians 15:6), and with James (see 1 Corinthians 15:7). For five to six weeks (forty days) after the Resurrection, Jesus met with and taught the Apostles and others, then said farewell from the Mount of Olives, near Bethany (see Luke 24:50–51; Acts 1:3–11). He appeared to Paul (see 1 Corinthians 9:1; 15:8), and again to John (see Revelation 1:9–18).

Jesus also visited personally with many righteous Nephite and Lamanite souls, as recorded in the Book of Mormon (see 3 Nephi 11:1–18:39), including another Quorum of Twelve Apostles in the western hemisphere (see 3 Nephi 27:1–28:12). Centuries later the resurrected Christ appeared to western hemisphere prophets Mormon and Moroni (see Mormon 1:15; Ether 12:39). In modern times he has appeared to Joseph Smith (see Joseph Smith—History 1:14–20) and to others.

APPEARANCES OF ADDITIONAL
RESURRECTED BEINGS

We do not know of the reality of the resurrection of the dead from the numerous appearances of Jesus Christ alone. Others have resurrected and shown themselves with their glorified, resurrected bodies also.

When the resurrected Moroni first manifested himself, Joseph Smith related in his history the most detailed descriptions of a resurrected person ever recorded (see Joseph Smith—History 1:30–32).

John the Baptist also appeared to Joseph Smith and Oliver Cowdery in a resurrected body, complete with the head that he had lost at the hands of Herod Antipas' executioner, showing that the miracle of resurrection restores body parts lost in mortality.

Then came Peter, James, and John—Peter and James returning to earth with resurrected bodies, but John with his translated or transfigured body.[11]

Other renowned ancient prophets came back to earth: Moses, Elias, and Elijah. Moses and Elijah had come back to earth eighteen hundred years earlier to the Mount of Transfiguration (see Matthew 17:3; Luke 9:30), but on that occasion they had returned to earth as translated beings,[12] since there was no resurrection from the dead at the time. Jesus Christ, as the scriptures attest, would be "the first-fruits of them that slept" (1 Corinthians 15:20), the first to resurrect from the dead to immortality (see Acts 26:23; Colossians 1:18; Revelation 1:5; 2 Nephi 2:8–9). On this latter-day occasion the two preeminent prophets came as resurrected beings, and on that same day the Lord Jesus Christ once again appeared to accept his house.

WHAT WE HAVE LEARNED ABOUT RESURRECTED BEINGS

From all these accounts—ancient and modern, on both hemispheres—we learn that Jesus Christ was the first of all who have ever lived on this planet to rise from the dead to immortality. Every human will resurrect, as Paul wrote: "As in Adam all die, even so in Christ shall all be made alive" (1 Corinthians 15:22), though not everyone will resurrect to the same glory: there are different levels or degrees of resurrected bodies, as the sun, moon, and stars differ from one another in glory (see 1 Corinthians 15:40–42). Resurrected bodies consist of more refined and pure physical/spiritual matter that can pass through what we regard as solid objects. They are composed of flesh and bone, but not blood (see Luke 24:39). They have power to eat and digest food (see Luke 24:43). They are tangible and corporeal (see Luke 24:39–40; John 20:25–29).

The Resurrection of the Lord, and our subsequent resurrection, is one of the most glorious messages of the gospel of Jesus Christ. Because of the gift of resurrection provided by our Savior, all humankind will rise again from the dead and live forever. In fact, there is no choice in the matter; as a gift from the God of heaven we are all going to live forever. The choice we do have is *where* and *with whom* we would like to live forever. We are now in the process of determining that by how we are behaving here on earth.

All consequences of the original Fall have been paid and resolved through our Savior's love. He loved us so much that he rescued us from our enemies, evil, death, and hell. This is the Father's great plan of happiness that his Firstborn Son championed. Elder Dallin H. Oaks declared:

> *The Resurrection of the Lord, and our subsequent resurrection, is one of the most glorious messages of the gospel of Jesus Christ.*

Many living witnesses can testify to the literal fulfillment of [the] scriptural assurances of the resurrection. Many, including some in my own extended family, have seen a departed loved one in vision or personal appearance and have witnessed their restoration in "proper and perfect frame" in the prime of life. Whether these were manifestations of persons already resurrected or of righteous spirits awaiting an assured resurrection, the reality and nature of the resurrection of mortals is evident. What a comfort to know that all who have been disadvantaged in life from birth defects, from mortal injuries, from disease, or from the natural deterioration of old age will be resurrected in "proper and perfect frame."

I wonder if we fully appreciate the enormous significance of our belief in a literal, universal resurrection.[13]

TESTIMONY OF THE RESURRECTION

Because the Ogden family lived in other, distant lands for many years as our children grew up, the children returned to America in the early 1990s never having attended a funeral service and never having seen a dead body. And I myself was nearly fifty years old before I ever *touched* a dead body. When David Galbraith and I were serving together in a BYU stake presidency, one of our high councilors died, and we went to his viewing. Standing over the casket, David gave me a little encouragement, and I touched the brother's hand. It still felt like flesh, but there was no warmth in the body at all—it was totally cold. I thought about that for a while. For many things to function these days, they have to be plugged in or connected to some power source, electricity or something else. Our bodies are self-contained, self-generating power sources; our brains and hearts and other systems keep our bodies on and operating. Our spirits are actually power sources; take them away and there is no life inside. Nothing works without the spirit. We say that we see with two eyeballs in the front of our heads, but if our spirits leave our bodies, those eyeballs won't see a thing. They don't work.

I testify that resurrection is real, for many have had personal experience with resurrected beings in our day, as documented in records of The Church of Jesus Christ of Latter-day Saints.

I believe that righteous men will, in a future day, use the priesthood and call spirits back into the bodies of their families—raising bodies into a permanently perfected condition.

And I testify that our Lord and Savior has manifested infinite love, kindness, and mercy by providing immortality and eternal life to every soul who really cares about him and his Father, and proves it by the way he or she lives. The greatest blessings in the universe, and the riches of eternity, are enumerated in the holy endowment that our Lord has revealed to us—in the initiatory or preparatory ordinances, in the instruction session with its veil ceremony, and in the sealing ordinances. In his holy house our Resurrected Savior most exquisitely continues to manifest his divine love for each of us.

NOTES

1. Howard W. Hunter, "An Apostle's Witness of the Resurrection," *Ensign*, May 1986, 16.

2. Orson F. Whitney, *Saturday Night Thoughts: A Series of Dissertations on Spiritual, Historical and Philosophic Themes* (Salt Lake City: Deseret News, 1921), 152.

3. F. F. Bruce, *New Testament History* (New York: Galilee Book, 1969), 206.

4. Ben Witherington III, *New Testament History—A Narrative Account* (Grand Rapids, MI: Baker Book House, 2001), 166.

5. Ben Witherington III, as cited in Lee Strobel, *The Case for Christ* (Grand Rapids, MI: Zondervan, 1998), 141.

6. The three persons Jesus raised from the dead were the son of the widow of Nain (Luke 7:11–17), the daughter of Jairus (Matthew 9:18–26; Mark 5:22–43; Luke 8:41–56), and Lazarus (John 11:1–46).

7. Bruce R. McConkie, *The Mortal Messiah*, 4 vols. (Salt Lake City: Deseret Book, 1979–81), 4:268.

8. *Teachings of Presidents of the Church: Joseph Smith* (Salt Lake City: The Church of Jesus Christ of Latter-day Saints, 2007), 211.

9. Robert J. Matthews, *Behold the Messiah* (Salt Lake City: Bookcraft, 1994), 280.

10. James E. Talmage, *Jesus the Christ* (Salt Lake City: Deseret Book, 1983), 633–34.

11. "The Latin *trans figura* (like the Greek *meta morpho*) means to change into another form. [At the Transfiguration, during Jesus' mortal ministry,] Peter, James, and John were transfigured, or changed, to another condition. . . . They passed into a higher state, but what is that state? The scriptures use a

number of terms to describe these changed beings: *transfigured* and *translated* are two of the descriptions, both meaning the same condition, though *transfigured* is short-term and *translated* is long-term. Other words used are 'renewed' and 'paradisiacal' (Article of Faith 10), 'caught up' (Moses 7:27; 3 Nephi 28:36; D&C 88:96), 'glorified' (Moses 1:11; 7:3), 'quickened' (D&C 67:11; 88:96), and 'changed in the twinkling of an eye' (3 Nephi 28:8; D&C 43:32, 63:51, 101:31). Most of these descriptions refer to the shifting upward from our current telestial condition to a terrestrial condition. To be transfigured or translated, then, means to be changed to a terrestrial level, where bodies (while in that condition) are sanctified, made holy, and do not experience mortal pains or death (3 Nephi 28:7–9, 13–17, 36–40). Transfiguration, or translation, Joseph Smith taught, 'is that of the terrestrial.'" D. Kelly Ogden and Andrew C. Skinner, *Verse by Verse: The Four Gospels* (Salt Lake City: Deseret Book, 2006), 339–40.

12. Moses and Elijah had both been translated upon concluding their mortal ministries so they could participate on earth in this very occasion of transfiguration. They were taken up, interestingly, in the same area east of the Jordan River opposite Jericho (see Deuteronomy 34:5; Alma 45:19; 2 Kings 2:11–12) where John the Baptist and Jesus both began their mortal ministries. Moses and Elijah "appeared in glory, and spake of his *death, and also his resurrection,* which he should accomplish at Jerusalem" (Joseph Smith Translation, Luke 9:31). Moses and Elijah were only six months away from their own potential resurrection and would understandably have been anxiously anticipating that glorious experience.

13. Dallin H. Oaks, "Resurrection," *Ensign*, May 2000, 15.

"WALK IN NEWNESS OF LIFE"

N othing is more beautiful than the beginning
of a new life. I cried and rejoiced at the birth
of each of our four children. A new baby is
so beautiful, so sweet, so tender. At such moments, the
veil between mortality and eternity seems almost trans-
parent and the love of God is unmistakable.

Likewise, I rejoice and get a little teary every time I
witness a renewal of spiritual life. How beautiful, how
sweet, how tender it is to see the heart changed, the
lost found, and the blind restored to sight. Though we
may not understand how it happens, we know why—
because God loves his children (see 1 Nephi 11:17).
Rebirth really is as precious as birth.

LLOYD D. NEWELL is a professor of Church history and
doctrine at Brigham Young University.

It seems fitting, then, that the Lord would use birth as a metaphor to describe the change that is made possible by the Atonement of Jesus Christ. We may smile when we read Nicodemus's bewildered question "How can a man be born when he is old? can he enter the second time into his mother's womb?" (John 3:4). But in our own way, we have all wondered the same thing. Can I really change? After all the mistakes I've made, can I really begin again? Is there hope for me—and for my loved ones?

We've all fallen short and longed for another chance, a fresh start, a new beginning. We've all wished we could rewind time and try again. We all have weaknesses that may at times feel like unshakable parts of our nature. We hear the expression "There are no guarantees in life." But here's a promise, a guarantee you can count on no matter where you are or what you have done: we *can* change; we *can* "walk in newness of life" (Romans 6:4).

That is the central message of the gospel, the doctrine of salvation, the whole point and purpose of life. In fact, it could be argued that this sublime truth *is* the gospel—the "good news" that Jesus Christ came to proclaim. Whenever God speaks to man—through his prophets or directly—his main message seems to be either that we *need* to change or that we *can* change.

My purpose today is to affirm just how anxiously our Heavenly Father wants us to believe that we can change. If the Atonement of Jesus Christ is the ultimate expression of

---

Right: Arnold Friberg, Alma Baptizes in the Waters of Mormon.

God's love—and I testify that it is—then another, equally powerful expression of that love is found in the many, varied ways in which he urges and encourages us to believe in the Atonement and access its power to change our lives.

THE NECESSITY OF CHANGE

When the Apostle Paul encouraged the Romans, and each of us, to "walk in newness of life" (Romans 6:4), he was speaking from firsthand experience. He knew what it was like to be born again. He was forever changed after his experience on the road to Damascus. That doesn't mean he was perfect or that he never sinned again, but something was certainly different after that experience that could justifiably be considered a rebirth. He was a new man—still just as zealous and committed a Christian as he had ever been as a persecutor, but now he walked with a power, light, and spirit that came from coming "alive unto God through Jesus Christ" (Romans 6:11). When he says, "Even so we also should walk in newness of life" (6:4), he is inviting us to walk with him in the converted newness he found in Christ.

Such references to "new life," along with the Lord's frequent invitations to be "born again," suggest something of the magnitude of change he has in mind for us. This isn't a tweak or a touch-up. The Atonement doesn't propose some minor alterations. This is a reset. It goes even deeper than changing our actions. Our nature, our disposition, and our whole worldview and mindset can become different—deeper, higher, holier.

But the magnitude of the change required should not discourage us. Heavenly Father knew from the beginning that sending his children into mortality surrounded by opposition meant that we would slip up, fall, and sometimes fail to get it right. But he bids us to take this walk anyway, because it is the only way we can continue to progress and ultimately become like him. It was never part of God's plan that we would stay the same. The Atonement of Jesus Christ saves us not by taking us back to where we once were but by taking us to better places that God has prepared for us. By accepting the Father's plan and rejecting Satan's, we recognized both the possibility that we would falter and the promise that we could progress— and we agreed with the Father that the chance of the latter was worth the risk of the former.

The rigorous change required by the gospel of Jesus Christ is . . . exciting and exhilarating! The plan of salvation is the ultimate adventure.

So you see, the rigorous change required by the gospel of Jesus Christ is not meant to be disheartening or exhausting; it's exciting and exhilarating! The plan of salvation is the ultimate adventure. Perhaps you don't think of yourself as adventurous, but you are! Sure, you could have chosen the easy path—Lucifer's assurance that, in exchange for your agency, he would make sure no one failed. But that was not for you! You stepped into the great unknown of mortality. You did it because you had faith in the Son of God and in the Father's plan for your happiness. Your testimony was what helped you conquer then, and it will help you conquer now (see Revelation 12:10–11).

Hope in Christ is at the heart of meaningful change. Our relationship with God is one of separation and restoration, of estrangement and reconciliation, of wandering and returning, of picking ourselves up when we have fallen, of accepting the heavenly power of the Savior's love and Atonement, and of trying again to live in harmony with higher ideals rather than lower impulses. President Ezra Taft Benson counseled: "We must be careful, as we seek to become more and more godlike, that we do not become discouraged and lose hope. . . . Hope is an anchor to the souls of men. Satan would have us cast away that anchor. In this way he can bring discouragement and surrender. But we must not lose hope. The Lord is pleased with every effort, even the tiny, daily ones in which we strive to be more like Him. Though we may see that we have far to go on the road to perfection, we must not give up hope."[1]

And let us remember that true conversion—walking in newness of life—is a lifelong process. Paul was not done after his transformative experience; even he had to stay with it, day after day, striving in righteousness. The Atonement works within each of us over time, little by little, day by day. This is why, in his loving mercy, the Lord commanded us to take the sacrament weekly. He knew that we would regularly need to repent, remember, and renew our covenants. Indeed, the walk in newness of life is a lifelong journey for all of us. Elder David A. Bednar explained it this way:

> Spiritual rebirth . . . typically does not occur quickly or all at once; it is an ongoing process—not a single event. Line upon line and precept upon precept, gradually and

almost imperceptibly, our motives, our thoughts, our words, and our deeds become aligned with the will of God. This phase of the transformation process requires time, persistence, and patience. . . . Our souls need to be continuously immersed in and saturated with the truth and the light of the Savior's gospel. Sporadic and shallow dipping in the doctrine of Christ and partial participation in His restored Church cannot produce the spiritual transformation that enables us to walk in a newness of life. Rather, fidelity to covenants, constancy of commitment, and offering our whole soul unto God are required if we are to receive the blessings of eternity.[2]

Rebirth, then, is not so much a moment as a mindset, an ongoing experience of the heart, or the gradual accumulation of countless righteous choices built up over a lifetime. It is a daily decision to sincerely accept the Lord's invitation to discipleship: "If any man will come after me, let him deny himself, and take up his cross daily, and follow me" (Luke 9:23). The path of discipleship becomes clearer the longer we stay on it; it is a process that takes patience. Our efforts and desires are known to the Lord; he sees our steps of faith and obedience and perseverance—however small and imperceptible they may seem at times. He knows our hearts, and we know enough of his heart to know that he loves us perfectly and continuously.

God often refers to us as his "little children,"[3] and he will patiently work with us as we falteringly try to emulate him, just as we work patiently with our own children. As Elder Neal A. Maxwell lovingly reminded us: "Our perfect

Father does not expect us to be perfect children yet. He had only one such Child. Meanwhile, therefore, sometimes with smudges on our cheeks, dirt on our hands, and shoes untied, stammeringly but smilingly we present God with a dandelion—as if it were an orchid or a rose! If for now the dandelion is the best we have to offer, He receives it, knowing what we may later place on the altar. It is good to remember how young we are spiritually."[4]

The purpose of life is to grow up—physically and spiritually. To do this, we must be tutored, identify our shortcomings, make course corrections, and get back more fully on the upward path of discipleship. Speaking of heaven, our postmortal estate, President Dieter F. Uchtdorf said, "Remember: the heavens will not be filled with those who never made mistakes but with those who recognized that they were off course and who corrected their ways to get back in the light of gospel truth."[5]

Will we recognize our need for the Savior, . . . or will we surrender to the pull of the world and the allurements of the adversary?

Of course, our Heavenly Father would prefer that we not commit sin in the first place, and the scriptures contain many warnings against seeking happiness in wickedness.[6] But he also knew that we would make mistakes and would need a Savior. He knows how great the distance is between where we are and where he is, and for that reason he wants us to believe we can really change.

So the question is not whether we will trip and fall, falter and stumble, but rather how we will respond when we do. Will we pick ourselves up, dust ourselves off, and try again? Or will we give in to despair and disillusionment? Will we recognize our need for the Savior, for renewal and redemption from this fallen state, or will we surrender to the pull of the world and the allurements of the adversary?

Elder Bruce C. Hafen put it this way: "If you have problems in your life, don't assume there is something wrong with you. Struggling with those problems is at the very core of life's purpose. As we draw close to God, He will show us our weaknesses and through them make us wiser, stronger. If you're seeing more of your weaknesses, that just might mean you're moving nearer to God, not farther away."[7]

THE POSSIBILITY OF CHANGE

In some ways, however, seeing our weaknesses is the easy part. The hard part is seeing a way out of them. We can recite the scriptures that speak of a mighty change of heart, putting off the natural man to become a Saint, and weak things being made strong (see Alma 5:14; Mosiah 3:19; Ether 12:27), but do we really know what that means? And do we really believe it—enough to actually experience the mighty change ourselves?

Knowing of our tendency to see things only as they are and not as they could be, the Lord seems to be using every possible means to teach us, persuade us, and lovingly convince us that we can change—that no matter what road we've been walking until now, we can indeed "walk in newness of life."

The events we celebrate at Eastertime provide an excellent example. It's surely no coincidence that the Savior's

sacrifice and Resurrection, complete with the promise
of renewed physical and spiritual life, occurred during
springtime. Who can witness the emergence of colorful
blossoms—on limbs that seemed so dead and barren all
winter—without marveling at the earth's miraculous re-
generation every year? The arrival of spring after a long,
cold winter is a bold declaration that rebirth is always
possible. It is an annual reaffirmation of our hope in new
life and renewed life, a sweet and tender reassurance of
hope centered in Jesus Christ. I suppose it shouldn't sur-
prise us that the Master Teacher uses the largest visual aid
in history—the world he created—to teach us about his
Atonement. Truly, "all things are created and made to bear
record" of him, including the marked change from winter
to spring (Moses 6:63).

When John the Baptist was preaching in the wilderness,
preparing the hearts of the people to receive the Messiah,
he quoted this passage from the writings of Isaiah: "Every
valley shall be filled, and every mountain and hill shall be
brought low; and the crooked shall be made straight, and
the rough ways shall be made smooth" (Luke 3:5; see also
Isaiah 40:4). Why this passage? What do valleys and mountains have to do with the Savior's impending ministry and
Atonement? It seems unlikely that John was talking only
about geography or topography. Perhaps these metaphors
tell us more about Jesus' mission than we might realize. It's
as if he were saying, "Change is coming. Think of something that seems permanent to you—like a mountain. That
mountain can be flattened. That's the degree of change
that is possible through the gospel of Jesus Christ. Are
there things in your life that seem insurmountable? They

Mountains in Phuchifha state at Chiangrai, Thailand. © *Phittavas Phupakdee*.

can be overcome. Does your life seem rough or unstable? Through the Atonement of Jesus Christ, all of that can be made smooth. Anything can change. You can change."

While life may be unpredictable and even unfair at times, Jesus Christ came to set it all right. Though you may have made mistakes that took you down a path you did not intend, Jesus Christ came to straighten it all out. He came to change things: darkness to light, evil to goodness, sickness to health, sorrow to joy, despair to hope.

Promises of change permeate the scriptures. Through Christ, sins that are red as blood can become white as snow (see Isaiah 1:18), death can lead to new life (see John 11:25–26), captives can be delivered (see Luke 4:18), the blind can see and the deaf hear (see Mosiah 3:5), those who mourn can be comforted (see Matthew 5:4), those who hunger and thirst can be filled (see Matthew 5:6), and the meek can be exalted and the proud made low (see Matthew 23:12).

So much of Christ's mortal ministry reinforces the doctrine of new life and new birth. Every time he healed someone who was lame or leprous, for example, not only was he giving that person a new life, but he was also teaching us about his ability to heal us spiritually. Consider the man sick with palsy whose friends lowered him through the roof of the house where Jesus was in hopes that the Savior would heal him. Obvious to everyone was the man's physical ailment, but clear only to the Savior were his spiritual needs, and that was what Jesus chose to address first. "Son, thy sins be forgiven thee," he said, to the disturbance of the observing Pharisees, who immediately accused Jesus of blasphemy. The Master's response revealed one of his purposes in healing the sick: "That ye may know that the

Son of man hath power on earth to forgive sins, . . . I say unto thee, Arise, and take up thy bed, and go thy way" (Mark 2:5–11). Of course, the Savior was interested in alleviating physical suffering, but he knew well that this was not his greatest power or most important mission. What he wanted most was to offer spiritual renewal, the transformation of the inner man and woman. He saw acts of physical healing as a way to impress upon our minds that he has power to heal us spiritually, to give us new life. Everything the Savior said or did—all of the changes he wrought—leads to the most important change of all: the one that occurs when a human soul "putteth off the natural man and becometh a saint" (Mosiah 3:19).

If you ever doubt that God can continue to love you when you have stumbled and made mistakes, if you ever question whether it is truly possible that God knows you individually, follow the example of Nephi, who said, "I know that he loveth his children; nevertheless, I do not know the meaning of all things" (1 Nephi 11:17). It is enough to know—and trust—that Heavenly Father and our Savior love us. The love of God is the most powerful force in the universe. Our Father loves us with a perfect, constant, and encompassing love. If we allow it to, his love will transform us.

Our Father loves us with a perfect, constant, and encompassing love. If we allow it to, his love will transform us.

Elder Russell M. Nelson sums it all up with this powerful witness: "We can change our behavior. Our very desires can change. How? There is only one way. True change—

permanent change—can come only through the healing, cleansing, and enabling power of the Atonement of Jesus Christ. He loves you—each of you! He allows you to access His power as you keep His commandments, eagerly, earnestly, and exactly. It is that simple and certain. The gospel of Jesus Christ *is* a gospel of change!"[8]

ALLOW OTHERS TO CHANGE

Most of us are familiar with Charles Dickens's *A Christmas Carol.* In this classic tale of redemption, the ghost of Jacob Marley, weighed down by the chains of selfishness he forged in life, visits his former business partner, the mean-spirited Ebenezer Scrooge, to warn him about the consequences of his miserly ways. Because Marley sets in motion a series of ghostly visitations, all is not lost for Scrooge, who sees his past, present, and future and undergoes a change of heart. This heartwarming story resonates with us because it reminds us so powerfully that anyone can change—even a callous old man who literally defines grumpy selfishness. If there's hope for Scrooge, there's hope for all of us.

But there is a tragic aspect to this story that never fully gets resolved. When you hear the word *scrooge,* what do you think of? Merriam-Webster's dictionary defines *scrooge* as "a miserly person."[9] Not "a person who was once miserly but who, when given a second chance, chose to reform his life and share his wealth with those less fortunate." Just "a miserly person." Even though everyone knows how Scrooge's story ends, his name has nevertheless entered our consciousness (and our dictionary) as the embodiment of what he once was—not what he ultimately

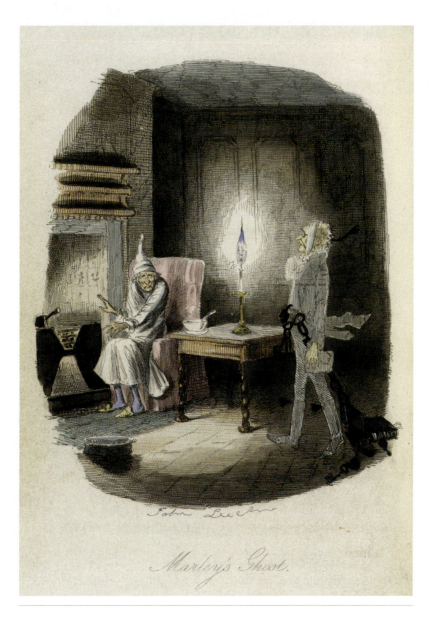

Jacob Marley's ghost visits Ebenezer Scrooge in Charles Dickens's A Christmas Carol, first edition, published by London-based Chapman & Hall in 1843. Illustration by John Leech. From the British Library's collections, 2013. Courtesy of Wikimedia Commons.

became. The poor Scrooge is immortalized for his abandoned past, not his reformed future.

Perhaps the way we remember fictional characters in
Christmas stories is of little consequence; however, the
way we think of our friends, neighbors, and family members is vital. Do we sometimes define people in terms of
who they have been rather than who they are or who they
can become? Our ability to accept change in our own lives
is tied, I believe, to our ability to accept it in the lives of
others.

Sometimes we stubbornly hold on to the past and re-
fuse to let others change and grow. Perhaps it is just a very
human tendency to remember people as we once knew
them. When Jesus instituted the sacrament among the
Nephites, he taught his disciples that they should not cast
out the unworthy or even the unrepentant. With encompassing love and an eternal perspective, the Lord exhorted
his disciples to pray for those people and continue to min-
ister to them, "*for ye know not* but what they will return
and repent, and come unto me with full purpose of heart,
and I shall heal them" (3 Nephi 18:32; emphasis added).
We just don't know what the future can bring and how
lives can change for the better. The final chapter is not yet
written on anyone's life. Elder Jeffrey R. Holland urged:

> Let people repent. Let people grow. Believe that people
> can change and improve. . . . If something is buried in
> the past, leave it buried. Don't keep going back with
> your little sand pail and beach shovel to dig it up, wave
> it around, and then throw it at someone, saying, "Hey!
> Do you remember *this*?" Splat!

Well, guess what? That is probably going to result in some ugly morsel being dug up out of *your* landfill with the reply, "Yeah, I remember it. Do *you* remember *this*?" Splat.

And soon enough everyone comes out of that exchange dirty and muddy and unhappy and hurt, when what our Father in Heaven pleads for is cleanliness and kindness and happiness and healing.[10]

Let us emulate the attitude of our patient, loving Father, described so beautifully by Elder Richard L. Evans: "Our Father in heaven is not an umpire who is trying to count us out. He is not a competitor who is trying to outsmart us. He is not a prosecutor who is trying to convict us. He is a loving Father who wants our happiness and eternal progress and who will help us all he can if we will but give him in our lives an opportunity to do so with obedience and humility, and faith and patience."[11]

Not long ago I was at the temple when an ordinance worker approached me to say hello. He said, "You don't recognize me, do you?" I glanced at his name badge, and memories started to form. He reminded me that he "was a rebel in high school." I began to remember him. I went to junior high and high school with him. I had not seen him since high school graduation decades earlier. With some chagrin, he acknowledged that he had been "wild and wayward" during those adolescent years. But now, here he was, nearly forty years later, an ordinance worker in the temple. He had a spiritual glow and warm happiness about him that inspired me and touched my heart. I thought, once more, how grateful I am for the gospel of Jesus Christ, the gospel of change and rebirth that empowers and enables us to "walk in newness of life."

President James E. Faust, in an article prepared shortly before he passed away, gave this encouraging counsel: "Each one of us has been given the power to change his or her life. As part of the Lord's great plan of happiness, we have individual agency to make decisions. We can decide to do better and to be better. . . . Each new day that dawns can be a new day for us to begin to change. We can change our environment. We can change our lives by substituting new habits for old. We can mold our character and future by purer thoughts and nobler actions. . . . Let us remember that the power to change is very real, and it is a great spiritual gift from God."[12]

Truly, nothing is more beautiful than seeing new life and renewed life. That hope and promise is centered in the Savior's encompassing love, and it is the sweetest, the most tender, and I think the most beautiful principle of the gospel.

May the Easter season reaffirm to our hearts and minds that lives can change, that people can change—they can even be reborn. Every time we see a spring flower, every time we read of the miracles of the Savior, every time we witness or participate in an ordinance of the gospel, and every time we see the miracle of spiritual rebirth in a loved one, let us receive the message our loving Heavenly Father is trying to send us: he wants us to change, he knows we can change, he has prepared the way for us to change, and he will help us "walk in newness of life," every step of the way.

NOTES

1. Ezra Taft Benson, "A Mighty Change of Heart," *Ensign*, October 1989, 2.

2. David A. Bednar, "Ye Must Be Born Again," *Ensign*, May 2007, 21.

3. See, for example, John 13:33; D&C 50:40–41; 61:36; 78:17.

4. Cory H. Maxwell, ed., *The Neal A. Maxwell Quote Book* (Salt Lake City: Bookcraft, 1997), 243.

5. Dieter F. Uchtdorf, "A Matter of a Few Degrees," *Ensign*, May 2008, 60.

6. See Isaiah 57:21; Psalm 32:10; Alma 41:10; Helaman 13:38; Mormon 2:13.

7. Bruce C. Hafen, "The Atonement: All for All," *Ensign*, May 2004, 97.

8. Russell M. Nelson, "Decisions for Eternity," *Ensign*, November 2013, 108; see also Mosiah 5:2; Alma 5:12–14; Moroni 8:17; Ether 12:33–34; D&C 138:4; Articles of Faith 1:3.

9. *Merriam-Webster's Collegiate Dictionary*, 11th ed., s.v. "scrooge."

10. Jeffrey R. Holland, "The Best Is Yet to Be," *Ensign*, January 2010, 26.

11. Richard L. Evans, as quoted by N. Eldon Tanner, in Conference Report, October 1967, 51.

12. James E. Faust, "The Power to Change," *Ensign*, November 2007, 122–24.

JENNIFER BRINKERHOFF PLATT

WALKING IN THE LIGHT
OF HIS LOVE

N ot long ago, on the campus of Brigham Young University, I was teaching a New Testament class focused on the life of Jesus Christ. At the conclusion of a discussion focused on the hypocrisy[1] of those that questioned the Savior's authority and the signs[2] given of his Second Coming, I had a student approach me to ask a question. His motive seemed pure as he reflected: "The scriptures state that in the last days, if it were possible, even the very elect will be deceived.[3] Sister Platt, how will I know him? I don't want to be deceived."

My first thought was to turn to the scriptures and reexplore what we had just studied in class pertaining to the signs of Christ's Second Coming. But the Spirit

JENNIFER BRINKERHOFF PLATT was a visiting assistant professor of ancient scripture at Brigham Young University.

prompted otherwise. Instead, I asked a question much like one the Lord has asked on various occasions: "Do you know him now? Is he familiar to you?" Or in the words of Jesus, "What think ye of Christ?"[4] His eyes filled with tears. "No. I don't think I know him as I should. Please teach me how I can come to recognize him." His honest inquiry is reflective of every disciple's desire. How can a sincere seeker of truth come to know and recognize Jesus Christ so he or she is not deceived?

Certainly we live in the last days and many are deceived, "for Satan is abroad in the land, and he goeth forth deceiving the nations."[5] Yet the role of the adversary is essential to agency. He is total darkness in contrast to the light of Christ's love. We can choose to walk in Christ's light. The Lord has established a pattern that, when applied, helps us to avoid deception. The promise is that those who "prayeth, whose spirit is contrite, the same is accepted of me if he obey mine ordinances. He that speaketh, whose spirit is contrite, whose language is meek and edifieth, the same is of God if he obey mine ordinances. And again, he that trembleth under my power shall be made strong, and shall bring forth fruits of praise and wisdom, according to the revelations and truths which I have given."[6] Simply stated, those that emulate the Savior by walking in the light of his love, observe God's covenants with real intent, and follow the Holy Ghost with humility will be protected from deception. The Savior establishes a pattern of obedience for us to follow.

Right: Harry Anderson, Sermon on the Mount. *© by Intellectual Reserve, Inc.*

OUR SAVIOR'S LOVE

EMULATING THE SAVIOR

Author Edward LeRoy Hart's text for the hymn "Our Savior's Love" illuminates a process for discerning truth from God. He reminisces that the inspiration for writing the words to the hymn grew out of a simile reflecting a simple, everyday observation: he had watched shoppers assess the true color of a piece of fabric by holding it up to the sunlight, as the natural light gives the most accurate representation of the color.[7] Likewise, the most accurate assessment of whether something is true or not is in the light of our Savior's love. When we hold our character to the light of the Son, he will show us the truth of who we are and correct our course so we can make adjustments to more accurately reflect his light. Our challenge is to prioritize our time to perform works in the natural light of the Lord rather than in artificial light of the adversary. As we seek daily to walk in the light of his love, we come to recognize him, know him, and pattern our lives after his works, while becoming worthy receptacles of his light.

General conference is a context for self-reflection, assessment, and increasing in light and knowledge. The words of living prophets and apostles draw clear and accurate light into our lives. When we study and review their teachings on a regular basis, we see specific ways to refine our discipleship. Choosing to act promptly on invitations given from the conference speakers will increase our awareness of the Spirit in our lives, while also refining and developing our character. An example of an invitation to act is found in the April 2014 general conference. Elder M. Russell Ballard invited the Church to study the missionary guide *Preach My Gospel*: "I invite all members, regardless

126

of your current calling or level of activity in the Church, to obtain a copy of *Preach My Gospel*. It is available through our distribution centers and also online. The online version can be read or downloaded at no cost. It is a guidebook for missionary work—which means it is a guidebook for all of us. Read it, study it, and then apply what you learn to help you understand how to bring souls to Christ through invitation and follow-up."[8]

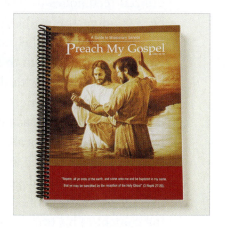

Preach My Gospel: A Guide to Missionary Service. © *by Intellectual Reserve, Inc.*

This tangible and measurable act has the potential to profoundly influence the lives of those who choose to obey. Not long after this invitation was extended, I chose to initiate a study of *Preach My Gospel*. This was something I had felt drawn to for years, yet it wasn't until Elder Ballard's invitation that I finally began to study the manual. I found myself particularly drawn to chapter 6, "How Do I Develop Christlike Attributes?," and the attribute activity found within that chapter.[9] This personal assessment invites us to reflect upon our fallen nature and how we can conquer the natural man through the Atonement of Christ by focusing on and seeking to acquire his attributes. Through my study of attributes such as faith, charity, humility, and hope, I recognize the intentionality of the Savior in his teachings. While being deliberate and purposeful is not one of the listed attributes in the manual,

I believe that the attribute of being intentional shapes all other Christlike attributes.

Exploring the various teaching methods[10] of the Messiah helps to illuminate his intentional and deliberate approach to life. As the Master Teacher, our Lord utilized techniques to best meet the needs of whomever he was interacting with. There were times when he used his surroundings to help others to understand what he was intending for them to learn. Ordinary circumstances became magnificent with the touch of the Master's hand. Questions invited learners to self-reflect and search for understanding. Miraculous healings evidenced his power to heal not only the physical but the spiritual ailments of broken souls. Objects such as nets, coins, wheat, and various other things anchored gospel truths in the visual memory. Likewise, the context of learning was as important as the content of his teachings. The Sermon on the Mount is more fully understood when we imagine gathering on the Galilean hillside that became the schoolroom for the autobiographical sketch written in his deeds.[11] Consider the profound meaning Jesus brought to the annual ritual of the feast of tabernacles. This joyous celebration included the lighting of four menorahs in the temple courtyard "to signify the covenant people's roles as the light unto the nations."[12] It was amid the brilliance of the four seventy-five-foot-high lighted menorahs that Christ declared, "I am the light of the world: he that followeth me shall not walk in darkness, but shall have the light of life."[13] This ritual now acclaimed meaning beyond an annual celebration to ignite the house of Israel to truly illuminate the world. Indeed, the Lord's previous teaching "Ye are the light of the world.

A city that is set on an hill cannot be hid. Neither do men light a candle, and put it under a bushel, but on a candlestick; and it giveth light unto all that are in the house. Let your light so shine before men, that they may see your good works, and glorify your Father which is in heaven"[14] becomes a call to come and fan the flame of our faith in the light of his love.

Jesus taught in parables to veil meaning and to give understanding to those with faith and intelligence sufficient to understand.[15] Likewise, our lives are living parables filled with experiences that can be viewed as either mere stories or customized tutoring, fitted for our own learning and understanding. Christ's teachings, like every moment of his life, are purposeful and focused on his mission of fulfilling the will of the Father by drawing men and women unto him so they might return to the Father.[16] Studying *Preach My Gospel*, particularly Christ's attributes, increases our desire to bring meaning to everything we do. When we seek to be like him, we will perform even menial tasks with greater intention.

KEEPING COVENANTS WITH REAL INTENT

Bringing meaning to our day-to-day tasks helps us to walk in the light of his love. I believe that many of us do good things every day but perhaps have become complacent and routine in our performance, forgetting to acknowledge or recognize the power of doing small and simple things with great meaning and purpose. For years now, I have studied the power of ritual and the impact intentionality has on the most mundane occurrences. Rather than performing

our day-to-day routines with little thought or effort, the most ordinary event can become rich in meaning. This is a practice of emulating Christ's approach to life by bringing purpose into the details of our life. We can ritualize the ordinary.

Rather than associate the word *ritual* with pagan ceremonies or animal sacrifices, consider a ritual as performing an act with sacredness by seeking for symbolic meaning. Rituals are a fundamental aspect of the ordinances and covenants associated with The Church of Jesus Christ of Latter-day Saints. Alonzo Gaskill, a researcher of rites and rituals, has noted:

> Mormons are traditionally not an extremely ritualistic people—at least not in their Sunday worship, nor in their day-to-day lives. Consequently, some find very little meaning in liturgy or ritual. Indeed, some saints struggle to "see symbolically," per se. One LDS scholar suggested that we Latter-day Saints "have become an asymbolic society, and, as a result, we do not understand the power of our own rites of passage. This same source added that most of us make little effort "to understand the meanings of our own rituals or what ritual behavior implies." Consequently, we fail "to comprehend or internalize the messages contained in ritual symbols."[17]

Seeking for meaning in rituals helps us to internalize the intent of Christ's message. Rituals lead us to conversion.

Left: Walter Rane, In Remembrance of Me. *© by Intellectual Reserve, Inc.*

Converted disciples walk in Christ's light and are not deceived.

Understanding how to approach a ritual helps us to make the ordinary into meaningful, symbolic experiences. According to Barbara Fiese,[18] a ritual is a symbolic event that has three fundamental parts: preparation for the event, participation in the event, and reminiscence of the event. These three elements of a ritual can (and often do) overlap, with participation being the predominant element. For instance, an individual may remember and reflect on past participation in a ritual while preparing for a future event. Within the context of a ritual, a group or community defines themselves and demonstrates their values and beliefs through the use of artifacts, symbols, and communication.[19]

Any ordinary occurrence can become sacred when the act is planned for, participated in with purpose, and then reminisced. This can be applied to making your bed, driving the car pool, studying for an exam, eating a meal with a loved one, studying the scriptures, praying—everything we do. We can emulate the life of the Master by doing ordinary things with great intent.

While all of Christ's deeds were purposeful, none were more meaningful than the final hours of his life. In his last twenty-four hours of mortality, he taught his disciples in a way to protect them and enlighten them for the remainder of their lives. In an upper room, he gathered his disciples for the most important Passover meal. This season for the Jews of recognizing the destroying angel passing over the children of Israel was about to take on new meaning as the Paschal Lamb was soon to be sacrificed for the salvation of every sinful soul. This ritual was planned for, participated in with great intention, and remembered by all who participated in it as well as any who read of the event.

The Lord's charge to "make ready"[20] the Passover meal included the attendance of a temple ceremony that prepared and slew a lamb. This ceremony included chanting passages from Psalm 81:

> Hear, O my people, and I will testify unto thee: O Israel, if thou wilt hearken unto me;
>
> There shall no strange god be in thee; neither shalt thou worship any strange god.
>
> I am the Lord thy God, which brought thee out of the land of Egypt: open thy mouth wide, and I will fill it.
>
> But my people would not hearken to my voice; and Israel would [have] none of me.
>
> So I gave them up unto their own hearts' lust: and they walked in their own counsels.
>
> Oh that my people had hearkened unto me, and Israel had walked in my ways![21]

Also included was the Hallel found in Psalm 113–18, with a response of "Save now, I beseech thee, O Lord: O Lord, I beseech thee, send now prosperity. Blessed be he that cometh in the name of the Lord."[22] Herbs and unleavened bread were acquired to make the meal complete. These preparations were vital for participating in the ritual.

Together the holy men (one being unholy) gathered in this final supper. In this setting, the Lord identified his betrayer, cast him out, then performed the ordinance. The attendees needed to be worthy of partaking of the supper, particularly because this meal was part of the important work of completing the law of Moses. As Elder Bruce R. McConkie taught:

> It is pleasant to suppose that this is the one Paschal supper over which Jesus presided, and that, therefore, he offered *the last symbolic sacrifice* preparatory to his offering of *the only real sacrifice* which would free men from their sins. If this is the case, the only sacrifices in which he involved himself (and there is a certain reverential fitness about such being the case) would be the symbolical one on Thursday whose emblems betokened the infinite and eternal one on Friday. Thus he would endorse and approve all of the similitudes of the past and announce their fulfillment in him. Thus also would the past, the present, and the future all be tied together in him, with the assurance held out to all the faithful of all ages, that all who look to him and his atoning sacrifice shall be saved.[23]

The ritual of the Last Supper was a preparatory ritual for the ultimate sacrifice described by Amulek in the Book of Mormon. This great and last sacrifice "bring[s] salvation to all those who shall believe on his name; this being the intent of this last sacrifice, to bring about the bowels of mercy, which overpowereth justice, and bringeth about means unto men that they may have faith unto repentance."[24]

Right: Del Parson, Jesus Washing the Feet of the Apostles.

© by Intellectual Reserve, Inc.

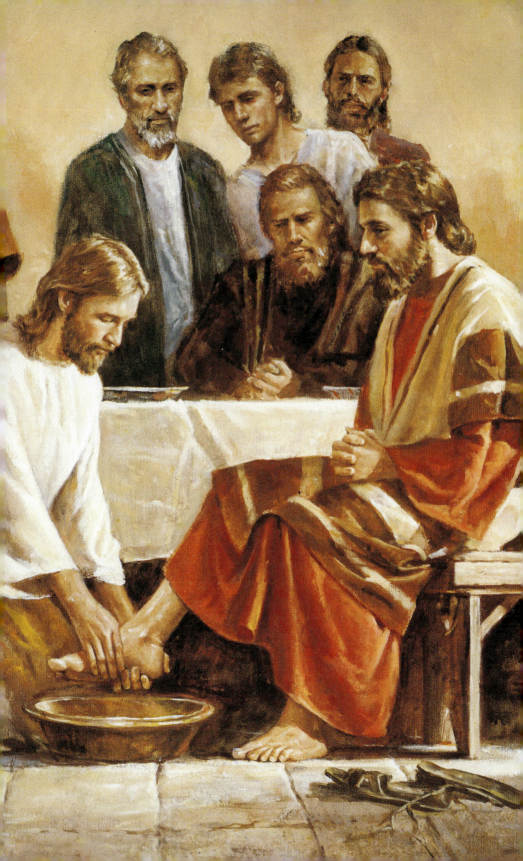

The sacrament was followed by the ordinance of washing feet and the teachings exclusive to John 13–17. The deliberate Messiah desired that his disciples be armed with righteousness, prepared for not only what the coming hours held for each of them but also for their lifetime of persecution. They needed his light in order to not be deceived. The fundamental themes of the teachings captured by John pertain to serving and loving one another,[25] showing love for the Lord by keeping the commandments, and preparing for the promised Comforter.[26] Using powerful symbols of a vine and branches, he assures them that their good works will be purged, tested, and pruned in order to bring forth more fruit.[27] Unlike the fig tree[28] that had been cursed days before, the Lord's disciples are invited to bring forth good works, to be fruitful. The great Intercessory Prayer[29] demonstrates the profound unity between the Father and the Son. Here the Lord commits to making an intercession for all; he accounts for his mortal mission and pleads for us to become one as he and the Father are one.

The deliberate Messiah desired that his disciples be armed with righteousness, prepared for not only what the coming hours held . . . but also for their lifetime of persecution.

The pinnacle of the Lord's mortal mission begins in the weary journey to the Mount of Olives, the place of Atonement. Every intentional deed he had performed in his lifetime prepared him for this singular experience. Yet his cognitive understanding of what he was to do did not match the experience.[30] Uttering words of submission and total surrender qualified him as the Savior of the world. With great drops of blood he bore the torment of pain, suffering, sin, and the calamity of every human soul.[31]

The all-night trials led him to Golgotha. Here the experience of Gethsemane was repeated as he hung on the cross and completed his work of redemption.[32] God the Father must have sequestered himself in the furthest corner of the universe during that unimaginably dark and lonely moment of death. "That the supreme sacrifice of the Son might be consummated in all its fulness, the Father seems to have withdrawn the support of His immediate Presence [while Jesus was on the cross], leaving to the Savior of men the glory of complete victory over the forces of sin and death."[33] Christ's willingness to have "trodden the winepress alone"[34] sheds the brightest and purest light on the human family in that brilliant and glorious moment of redemption.

We commemorate and reignite this redemptive light in our weekly ritual of the Passover. The sacrament is our reminder of his sacrifice as we renew our covenantal commitment to walk with him. But does routine participation negate our opportunity for communion with the Lord? How can we approach this invitation to the Lord's Supper with greater intention, performing it as a sacred ritual, rich in symbolic meaning? First we must come to understand the richness of its meaning. Elder Jeffrey R. Holland has taught:

> Perhaps we do not always attach that kind of meaning to
> our weekly sacramental service. How "sacred" and how

"holy" is it? Do we see it as *our* passover, remembrance of *our* safety and deliverance and redemption?

With so very much at stake, this ordinance commemorating our escape from the angel of darkness should be taken more seriously than it sometimes is. It should be a powerful, reverent, reflective moment. It should encourage spiritual feelings and impressions. As such it should not be rushed. It is not something to "get over" so that the real purpose of a sacrament meeting can be pursued. This *is* the real purpose of the meeting. And everything that is said or sung or prayed in those services should be consistent with the grandeur of this sacred ordinance.[35]

These few minutes each week are among the most significant rituals we participate in as Latter-day Saints. How then do we prepare for it and participate in it with greater intention? While we are not required to slay a lamb or gather herbs and unleavened bread, ours is a careful preparation measured in our deeds and efforts to remember all that we have promised to do. The passage of time between the partaking of sacrament from Sunday to Sunday is a cycle of preparation and remembrance. This is sacramental living. President Joseph Fielding Smith teaches that the sacrament is a renewal of our covenants and thus an incentive for righteousness.[36] We measure our faith by our works. Thus our desires to prepare for the sacrament are performed with great faith, remembering the works of Jesus Christ and seeking to pattern our lives after his.

If a man fully realized what it means when he partakes of the sacrament, that he covenants to take upon him the name of Jesus Christ and to always remember him and keep his commandments, and this vow is renewed week by week—do you think such a man will fail to pay his tithing? Do you think such a man will break the Sabbath day or disregard the Word of Wisdom? Do you think he will fail to be prayerful, and that he will not attend his quorum duties and other duties in the Church? It seems to me that such a thing as a violation of these sacred principles and duties is impossible when a man knows what it means to make such vows week by week unto the Lord and before the saints.

If we have the right understanding, we will live in full accord with the principles of truth and walk in righteousness before the Lord. How can we receive his Spirit otherwise? I can see the significance in the commandment the Lord has given us to assemble frequently and partake of these emblems in commemoration of his death. It is our duty to assemble and renew our covenants and take upon us fresh obligations to serve the Lord.[37]

The Holy Ghost guides and directs our preparations as we remember our covenants. It is a beautiful cycle of preparing and remembering, the two working in tandem. We can prepare specifically and deliberately in the hours and moments prior to partaking of the emblems of the sacrament. Elder Russell M. Nelson of the Quorum of the Twelve Apostles taught: "We commemorate His Atonement in a very personal way. We bring a broken heart and a contrite spirit to our sacrament meeting. . . . This is not a time for conversation or transmission of messages but a period of prayerful meditation as . . . members prepare spiritually for the sacrament."[38] Disciplining ourselves with quiet self-reflection transforms the power of the ritual. Ours is the offering of a broken heart and contrite spirit, the requirement the Lord requested of the Nephites with the completion of the law of Moses. The way we converse and communicate is a reflection of the value we place on the covenant we have renewed. We seek to mourn with those that mourn, to comfort, to bless, and to lift. This is demonstrated in the example of Sister Susan Bednar, wife of Elder David A. Bednar. Elder Bednar notes:

Disciplining ourselves with quiet self-reflection transforms the power of the ritual. . . . Our preparation for the sacrament shapes the way we live our covenants.

Before attending her sacrament meetings, Sister Bednar frequently prays for the spiritual eyes to see those who have a need. Often as she observes the brothers and sisters and children in the congregation, she will feel a spiritual nudge to visit with or make a phone call to a particular person. And when Sister Bednar receives such an impression, she promptly responds and obeys. It often is the case that as soon as the "amen" is spoken in the benediction, she will talk with a teenager or hug a sister or, upon returning home, immediately pick up the phone and make a call. As long as I have known Sister Bednar, people have marveled at her capacity to discern and respond to their needs. Often they will ask her, "How did you know?" The spiritual gift of being quick to observe has enabled her to see and to act promptly and has been a great blessing in the lives of many people.[39]

Our preparation for the sacrament shapes the way we live our covenants. Coming to the feast of the Lord's Supper each week with a desire to act in faith demonstrates our willingness to always remember him and thus do as he would do if he were here among us.

FOLLOWING THE SPIRIT WITH HUMILITY

Similarly, the way we participate in the actual rite matters very much. While the prayers and administration of the sacrament are prescribed, our receiving of the sacrament is not prescriptive. In those brief moments, we are invited to ponder the magnitude of the Atonement while making our own sacrificial offering in the similitude of the Son: the offering of contrite brokenness. This is a moment of absolute focus and fixed determination to ponder anew what the Almighty can do.[40]

The actual participation in the ritual is brief. Thus the prospect of reminiscing is expanded by continually preparing for the next opportunity to worship in the ritual of the sacrament. In the case of this practice, the remembering is bound with a promise. In our willingness to strive to always remember him and keep his commandments, we are promised to have his spirit to be with us always.[41] This promise should be taken at face value. We are intended to have the constant companionship of the Holy Ghost, the third member of the Godhead, with us always.

Establishing a priority of seeking the constant companionship of the Holy Ghost should be of utmost importance as he helps us to order the demands of our daily life. In that upper room setting, the Savior promised, "But the Comforter, which is the Holy Ghost, whom the Father will send in my name, he shall teach you all things, and bring all things to your remembrance, whatsoever I have said unto you. Peace I leave with you, my peace I give unto you: not as the world giveth, give I unto you. Let not your heart be troubled, neither let it be afraid."[42] The Holy Ghost's mission is to testify of Jesus Christ and the Atonement. He bears witness of the pure light of Jesus Christ, the Prince of Peace and our source of absolute truth.

This experience of ritualizing the sacrament has been a blessing in my life. Not long ago I had a profound experience with partaking of the emblems of the sacrament. On this particular Sunday I needed to be in two places at the same time: a ward conference and a Primary children's sacrament meeting presentation. I knew I could figure out how to juggle both events but decided to pray to know where I should be. The answer was simple and came as a thought: the name of a man in our stake that was in a serious battle with cancer came to mind. He lives in the ward that was having their ward conference. I went to his ward.

As I sat in the back of the chapel contemplating the prompt to be there, I found myself filled with emotion. While I did not see this man in the congregation, I felt grateful that I had acted in obedience to the simple prompting. We were singing one of my favorite sacrament hymns, "In Humility, Our Savior." The words penetrated my heart:

In humility, our Savior,
Grant thy Spirit here, we pray,
As we bless the bread and water
In thy name this holy day.
Let me not forget, O Savior,
Thou didst bleed and die for me
When thy heart was stilled and broken
On the cross at Calvary.

Fill our hearts with sweet forgiving;
Teach us tolerance and love.
Let our prayers find access to thee
In thy holy courts above.
Then, when we have proven worthy
Of thy sacrifice divine,
Lord, let us regain thy presence;
Let thy glory round us shine.[43]

My whole soul seemed to be responding to the pleas of this song. I found myself reflecting on the Atonement and my opportunity to change. I desired to understand more of the humility of our Savior. My heart desired an example, a visualization of humble service. In those first moments of the passing of the sacrament, I heard someone coming into the chapel. At the door was my friend, the man whose name had come to my mind that morning. He required the help of his brother and a walker. This man who was facing death slowly made his way to take his position at the right of the bishop, as he was serving as a counselor in the bishopric. I watched him struggle, unable to move on his own. I marveled as he took the steps to the rostrum. He didn't